Proposition Fourteen

A Secessionist Remedy

Proposition·Fourteen
A Secessionist Remedy

by

Richard Cummings

THE
PERMANENT PRESS

Sagaponack, New York 11962

THE PERMANENT PRESS
Sagaponack, NY 11962

When you have reached the edge of the abyss, the only thing that makes sense is to step back.

Alwyn Rees

Acknowledgments

Permission to reprint excerpts from the following books, periodicals and newspapers is to be acknowledged:

The East Hampton Star; Grit; *Community Politics,* Peter Hain, ed., John Calder (Publishers) Ltd. 1976; William Geekie, *Why Government Fails,* Libra Publishers, P.O. Box 165, 391 Willets Road, Roslyn Heights, L.I., N.Y. 11577 (1976); New York Magazine, "Who Runs the Subways" by Phillip Karp, April 9, 1979; The New Yorker, Richard Rovere, Nov. 9, 1978; *Democracy in America,* Volume 1, by Alexis de Tocqueville, translated by Henry Reeve, revised by Francis Bowen and edited by Phillip Bradley, Copyright, 1945 by Alfred A. Knopf, Inc.; Everett T. Rattray, *The South Fork,* Random House, 1979, Copyright by Everett T. Rattray; Charles Nordhoff, *The Communist Societies of the United States,* Schoken Books, 1965; Suffolk Life; *Volume One: Sunday Morning Services on the Farm* by Stephen Gaskin, Copyright 1977 by The Book Publishing Company, 156 Drakes Lane, Summertown, TN 38483; The Southampton Press; The New Republic, "There's Hope for Ethiopia," by Louis Rapoport, Feb.24, 1979; Yankee Inc., "A Bumper Sticker Affair, Mostly" by Henry Beetle Hough.

Credit for reprinting must be given the New York Times, Copyright 1972, 1978, 1979 by The New York Times Company. Reprinted by permission.

TABLE OF CONTENTS

INTRODUCTION

When I was asked to write this book, I hesitated because I thought American politics had become so hopeless, there seemed no positive suggestions I could make toward improving things. Then I began to think about how big America had grown and that to make it more human and less impersonal, perhaps we could begin to scale it down; break it up into smaller units.

Many Americans may encounter difficulties accepting the fact that we no longer need such a huge government establishment. Cuts in spending and in the federal budget will hurt or inconvenience many individuals and institutions that have lived off these publicly provided funds for years. Eventually, though, the budget will be reduced considerably—if for no other reason than our inability to afford it any longer. As the giant state begins to erode, one wonders what will replace it.

From my reading and almost daily newscasts, it was increasingly evident that people in other countries were also having difficulties dealing with their governments; Witness the Kurdish people's desire to secede from Iran once the Shah was deposed. Formerly suppressed, they now insisted upon autonomy. Ever since Francisco Franco died, the same process has occurred in Spain where Basques, Catalonians, and Andalusians increasingly assert and insist upon some form of independence from Madrid. And in Quebec, French Canadians seek freedom from Ottawa.

Here at home, people have begun to rebel against higher taxes and we see similar demands for autonomy. One word coming back into vogue is "secession." Another (spoken by Puerto Rican nationalists) is "independence."

My negative perceptions of this process began to change as I slowly came to appreciate the constructive aspects of this "rebellion." The major political parties, not having responded to the needs or desires of most Americans have forced citizens to start acting independently. This has led to a clear revival of direct democracy through the use of Initiative and Referendum.

The most striking example of this phenomenon was Proposition 13 in California. Howard Jarvis, a man in his seventies, organized and led a tax revolt which culminated in a referendum, passed by popular vote, which slashed property taxes by sixty percent. Since then the process of Initiative and Referendum has been used in connection with other issues —such as rent control, limiting state government spending, legalizing marijuana usage—and many communities are demanding the adoption of these procedures so that their citizens can accomplish what their legislators will not.

Moreover, in recent years, angry Americans have begun demanding the recall of elected officials who have proved inept or faithless. Also, increasingly, communities have sought to break away from larger entities to form their own towns, countries, or states. In Maine there is even talk of leaving the country altogether, while the American Indians insist they never joined.

What does all this mean? Taken together, these recent developments in political awareness and citizen activism seem to constitute the first steps beyond Proposition 13. The growing demand is for local autonomy for individual communities; independence for the many small "nations" which comprise America. This heralds a return to the renaissance of direct democracy, as originally practiced in the Town Meetings of New England, before the United States even existed.

The idea might seem far-fetched or even frightening, but it is an idea that is gaining strength. Something is stirring. I have tried to explain what it is and why it is happening. I am now fairly optimistic about it, and have concluded that most Americans will be too, once they grasp that a restoration of true democracy is in their own self (and community) interest.

My sources have been mostly newspapers: *The New York Times*, *The East Hampton Star*, *The Amsterdam News*, among others. This is virtually a day to day phenomenon and must be appreciated as such. Any number of books, especially *Community Politics*, edited by Peter Hain, have been useful, as have numerous articles and essays written by Karl Hess. Everett Rattray's *South Fork* gave me an understanding of the nature of independence in small towns before the American

Revolution, as have James Truslow Adams' *History of South-hampton* and Alexis De Tocqueville's *Democracy in America.* I am indebted, as well, to the magazine *Undercurrents* and numerous interviews and private letters.

Clearly, a serious malady affects the nation. Symptoms erupt continually. Those who feel themselves disenfranchised react with listless acceptance or feverish outbreaks of rage. Neither response tends to make for a sound society.

I've tried to focus on those recuperative forces within the nation, working independently, which are acting to redress local grievances. Those efforts which give the promise of renewed health all seem to point in the direction of community autonomy, for it is only when ultimate decision-making returns to a neighborhood that citizens can again control their destinies and the quality of their lives. Ironically, this call for returning power to the cities and townships of America—to a vision of a nation made up of independent communities—harks back to America's starting point.

How far will this movement go? Frankly, it's anybody's guess. But I should imagine that it will go just so far as we dare it.

Richard Cummings
Bridgehampton, N.Y.
May, 1980

PART ONE

EXAMINATION AND DIAGNOSIS

I. INSTITUTIONAL TORPOR

Many Americans rue the passing of the family farm, sold off to developers, subdivided, replaced by the giant miasma of unplanned growth. Ed Zebrowski is a farmer in Bridgehampton, Long Island. He farms his own land and his broad grin and burly physique reflect the pleasure he finds in his life's work. Right now, though, Ed Zebrowski has a problem. The Departments of Agriculture of both New York State and the federal government require his growing Hudson potatoes on a predetermined portion of his land. Supposedly, Hudsons are resistant to golden nematode, which is the major crop pest on eastern Long Island. Ed believes he can control the pest organically—without resorting to the poisonous spraying the Government does.

Each year, officials of the U.S. Department of Agriculture take samples of the farm land, and if they find any soil infestation, they order that land withdrawn from farming and fumigated. Then, the Government compensates the farmer at the rate of $60 an acre for the unused land—a figure arrived at shortly after World War II. As a food crop, potatoes can be grown in infested areas and still be perfectly safe to eat. Unless they are, however, of the nematode-resistant variety demanded by the federal and state governments, they are subject to quarantine.

This arrangement has one big flaw. The farmer cannot market the Hudson well, as it is of an inferior quality. In today's market, it's simply not a competitive product. Public agencies won't buy it nor will military installations, hospitals or prisons. According to Tony Tiska, a second generation Bridgehampton farmer:

> The nematode is not a serious threat to potato production. But the nematode-control program poses all kinds of problems for the farmer because once you're under the quarantine, the Government has essentially taken away a lot of your freedom to make decisions, and you can't run a business if you're not free to decide certain things![1]

Tiska, Zebrowski and others are trying to force the Government to make farm programs more responsible and flexible. But, as Tiska told *The Times*: "We've been to lawyers and they've told us, 'Forget it, you haven't got a chance. It's Federal law and you can't fight it. They've got you!'"

Because of the Hudson requirement, Zebrowski farms at a loss; meanwhile, his heavy land taxes continue to rise. Ed says he could grow other kinds of potatoes which would sell and be pest-resistant, but he isn't allowed to do so. The very Government he supports with tax dollars is forcing him to grow a crop, which even the Government won't buy. Zebrowski has always been a good-natured, hard-working man of the land. But now he has begun developing his property. Others have refused to sign the Government's quarantine agreement, preferring to incur the cost of fumigation themselves.

This situation is not unique. Bureaucratic convolution pervades virtually every segment of society. Businessmen are required to fill out so many forms they have no time to do business. Retired people wait months for Social Security checks, which are usually ensnarled in arcane technicalities or computer bogdowns. Companies are bombarded with federal, state and local regulations, which arrive unaccompanied by any guidelines for compliance.

Government agencies which promulgate this confusion are costly. Deficits in many state and city governments mount while agencies proliferate, their budgets increasing. Congress has been forced to raise the national debt limit by $30 billion in order to pay the cost of federal operations. Yet, despite incredibly large expenditures and burgeoning numbers of agencies, it is almost impossible for citizens to get action. A recent television news item illustrated this dilemma.

A number of homes in California were in imminent danger from a boulder tottering at the edge of a cliff above them. Threatening to fall at any moment, it would undoubtedly kill anyone in its path. Despite numerous calls to various agencies nothing had been done, as each agency referred the complainants to another department. One irate citizen complained: "You have to get through so many people and so many bureaucracies to get something done, even with human life at stake." Government bureaucracy, by its very size and complicated nature, defeats its intended purpose.

When Jimmy Carter was elected President, he resolved to reduce the size of the Federal Government. His first move was to create a commission of 175 people who were to study how this was to be accomplished. Its first report: a request for 90 additional people.

John Herbers has written:

> Americans believe that the Washington apparatus has a life of its own, that it does not matter who is in or out of power. The Federal bureaucracy absorbs all invaders, spinning more soft silk about its cocoon.[2]

Ralph Nader and Mark Green charge that in the private sector as well, bigness produces cumbersome inefficiency. Frederick Schere, an economist whose work has influenced Nader and Green, conducted 86 interviews with business managers, and concluded: " . . . the unit cost of management, including the hidden losses due to delayed or faulty decisions and weakened or distorted incentives . . . tend to rise with organizational size."[3]

William J. Geekie, in *Why Government Fails*, admonishes that this state of affairs allows the introduction of spurious forms of technology without any human consideration. For example, the horror of nuclear testing; a prime example of bureaucratic decision making with no thought being given to the people who will be most immediately and directly affected.

Huge enterprises, either in the public or the private sector, are run on bureaucratic principles which are fundamentally anti-democratic, particularly as they stifle free expression. It is not surprising, then, that they become unmanageable and obsolete in their gargantuan proportions. Vast institutions are incapable of give-and-take informal decision making or spontaneity. People within them communicate by memo—written, usually, in "in-house" code. Policy decisions and procedures emanate from the top and are accepted as gospel. The person at the peak of the corporate or bureaucratic ladder is czar, and, as such, is automatically right. Those below him either agree or are wrong. There is virtually no internal criticism. This is the principle of hierarchical infallibility, and a whistle-blower had better have an independent income.

The rote numbness which pervades bureaucracy causes people to lose their sense of what is right and wrong or even what is likely to happen. Thus, they become unthinking robots who, knowing their expected demeanor, and protecting their livelihoods, operate as mindless functionaries. Describing the Pentagon, Russell Baker has written:

> Indeed, the cunning loafer may find life safer than the aggressive take-charge guy so esteemed in the mythology of American free enterprise, since too much imaginative creativity may offend a bureaucracy that puts a high premium on quiet loyalty.[4]

Not so long ago, individuals or families owned the businesses in a community. They also lived there. As Oliver Larson, Executive Vice President of the Portland, Oregon Chamber of Commerce, put it:

> The biggest difference between now and the old days is in response to community needs. Then, some war horse would call a meeting of the people who decided things and it would get done. Now, they all have to contact corporate headquarters, at somewhere like Gravelswitch, Kansas, and it takes forever to get an answer.[5]

Just as big government usurps the role of small, local government, big business gobbles up small, locally controlled businesses. Despite Antitrust legislation, the acquisition trend is apparent everywhere. A local, family-owned department store is taken over by a national chain; a national newspaper takes over the local weekly. Overnight, it seems, local control gives way to a distant, impersonal authority. Suddenly, community sensibilities and furtherance bow to those of a multinational corporation. The executives transferred to a locality have little or no concern for the community. Rather, it serves as a temporary home within their greater fixation for the company and their own careers. Nader and Green have observed:

> Absentee corporations can decide not merely that a plant is not making money, but that it is not making enough money as compared to another profit center in the world-wide enterprise. Hence an executive in New York City or Brussels might decide to pull the plug on a facility in Youngstown, Ohio, in a way that local ownership with local allegiance would be unlikely to do.[6]

This distance equally infests big government. As remote

agencies take over the functions of local government, it becomes increasingly difficult to get any response. Mr. Geekie tells us, " . . . our public institutions are large, complex, and very fouled up."[7] Bureaucrats in Washington cannot be vitally concerned with the effects of legislation on the citizens of Carrollton, Georgia. They function within the parameters and under the pressures of their own careers and sponsors.

It must be noted as well, that American labor unions suffer from the same disease. They have grown to such size that their rank and file members have very little say over union policy. Union executives maneuver easily within the overall power establishment in this country and play a major role in many of the important decisions, affecting not only their union members, but everyone else in the country. Their views count, whether pertaining to the construction of nuclear power plants, the methods for combatting inflation, or the selection of Presidential candidates. In terms of personal power, George Meany was certainly on a par with Jimmy Carter or David Rockefeller.

This country grew to its present size and complexity over a scant two centuries; territorial expansion, mass immigration and the rapid rise of industrialism taking their toll. As a result, the Government grew in equal measure to correct the abuses stemming from racism, segregation and the manifold injustices of industrial interests. We were determined that workers and minorities be protected from short-sighted, powerful forces.

Alpheus T. Mason, Professor Emeritus of Princeton, has observed that Congress tried to deal with America's social problems through enactment of legislation. That engendered the bureaucracies. They, in turn, needed to be funded. He believes that these developments have brought on a major historical impasse: the clash between the mushrooming "Imperial Bureaucracy," and a taxpaying electorate which resents the bureaucracy's high cost. Mason acknowledges that no one understands the meaning of most of the social legislation enacted. To readily define it requires long, costly litigation. More important, Congress, believing that excessive clarity is politically dangerous, deliberately encourages interpretive confusion.

Congress is not alone. Agencies, too, have accrued and maintained their power by adopting complex regulations. Said Geoffrey C. Hazard, of Yale Law School: "The regulatory agencies have a great appetite for novelty. They're imperialists; . . ."[8] always seeking to expand their functions, staff and size.

There is another significant factor in our growth: the U.S. role as global policeman and defender of freedom. In this capacity, we have necessitated an enormous defense budget and very sophisticated weapons systems, which experts now say we don't have the manpower to utilize. Sharing our military systems with allies in the Third World has proved an actual impediment to world peace. As the Vietnam War amply showed, underdeveloped countries can't use our surplus arms any more successfully than we can. What's more, our armaments often end up in the hands of unstable figureheads—even tyrannical ones—who make war or promote unrest at the direction of their own whims. Meanwhile, we continue to sign costly defense contracts to amass useless additional weaponry, or merely to tide over floundering corporations within the military-industrial complex.

Admiral Rickover shrewdly noted that America provides socialism for the upper class and free enterprise for the middle and lower classes. He suggested that, in effect, defense contracts subsidize giant corporations with money accrued from ordinary working people—people whose income is in no way subject to such government assistance. Thus, the Government short changes the individual citizen in the pursuit of its own power-oriented priorities.

One of the largest bureaucracies in the Federal Government is the greater State Department, with all of its attendant bodies and ancillary agencies. When Thomas Jefferson was Secretary of State, he presided over some thirty people. Today, hundreds of thousands of people are involved in the study, planning and administration of U.S. foreign policy. It is absolutely impossible—given the overlap and entanglement of functions—for the right hand to ever know what the left is doing. This is a treacherous context within which to determine and manage the U.S. position in today's terribly complex and sensitive world. The result is that in addition to operating at cross purposes, outright ignorance abounds.

I once attended a staff meeting of the Agency for International Development, where the topic was Yemen. The top administrator did not know facts about the situation which had been on the front page of that day's *New York Times*. That I was privy to the information astonished him, so I produced the paper and pointed to the article.

Later, wandering through the hallways of the State Department, I came across an office door plaque which read: "Deputy Assistant to the Assistant Administrator for Administration." *Who* is the mysterious occupant of this esoteric position? *What*, in God's name, does he do? If one could examine him at work, the chances are that he would be found behind an uncluttered desk and staring out the window. Over-educated, under-utilized, but gainfully employed.

Under the aegis of this monstrous bureaucracy, American foreign policy is in shambles. When Professor Richard Gardner, of Columbia Law School, presently Ambassador to Italy, served as Deputy Assistant Secretary for International Organization Affairs, he complained that before a cable could be sent, it was rewritten a dozen times, then approved by about twenty different offices. In an urgent situation, swift response is therefore utterly impossible. This incredible duplication of effort is, to some extent, the result of each individual section's inherent knowledge of its own expendability. Each one must appear to have a function, even if there are dozens of other entities performing the identical function. Thus, since Thomas Jefferson's day, self-servers have replaced visionaries in the seats of power.

In addition to self-protection through duplication of effort, bureaucracy produces a deleteriously self-interested gutlessness—in short, an absolute lack of vision. This is evident in both the private and public sectors. As any banker knows, a loan officer is far more disposed to refuse a loan to a new business than to approve it. The only sure way for an applicant to get a loan is not to need it in the first place, for if the borrower defaults, the loan officer will be blamed. (The officer, however, receives no particular accolades in the event that the venture proves successful.) Therefore, the banker faces a non-decision: refuse the loan, and be assured of regular, automatic raises and advancement, or approve it, and risk the disapproval of superiors—perhaps even the loss of his job. The usual answer: play it safe.

Like business enterprises, government agencies arrive at decisions by relying upon established procedure and information, supporting conclusions long since determined. Job protection is no small factor in this practice with risk or innovation being nothing short of astonishing. The result? Hackneyism and stagnation. Undoubtedly, this underlies America's current technological lag. In today's world, Thomas Edison would quite probably have been stopped cold. Capital for a new idea is scarce. Despite all of our know-how, little or no backing has been forthcoming for an automobile which uses less gas or works on a system other than internal combustion. It is easier—"safer"—for the Government and utilities to cooperate in the construction and operation of nuclear power plants, despite the imminent danger to the citizenry, than to capitalize the development of alternate energy sources.

The drones of corporate and government complexes hold their loyalty to the institution or organization—not to a real community. Thus, they form a kind of supra-community apart, and see all the world around them as existing for their own use and benefit.

This pattern easily absorbs elected officials. Legislative bodies are thoroughgoingly bureaucratic. Problems are referred to committees for study and recommendation, and the resultant studies and recommendations are often filed and forgotten. Obeisance must be paid to "higher-ups," and the best way to keep one's job and expect advancement is to avoid controversy, to play the game by established rules.

As long as decision makers in the private and public sectors continue to put job security ahead of real creativity and problem solving, they are not serving the public. As capitalists they impede, if not prevent, free enterprise. As public officials, they participate in a democracy in name only.

Americans are beginning to realize that they must regain

control, and that one path is the reduction in size of many societal institutions. Local autonomy is part of this process. So begin the processes of "smalling down" and decentralization.

II. LAND SICKNESS

I'm scared to death," announced Hilda Lyte of Middletown, Pennsylvania[9] —so scared that she wouldn't drink milk from her own cows. It might have been contaminated by the radioactivity coming from the Babcock & Wilcox nuclear power plant at Three Mile Island. The accident which *couldn't* happen, did. There was the very real and horrifying possibility of a meltdown.

Middletown is exactly what the name implies: a middle-American community of down-to-earth, sensible people, who work for a living. The population is 12,000—400 of whom are black. In defiance of social stereotype, Middletown elected Bob Reed, a black man, mayor.

Suddenly, Bob Reed, Hilda Lyte, and all the other people of Middletown learned about radioactive Xenon gas and Iodine 131 in the Susquehanna River—practically in their backyards. This explained why the Metropolitan Edison Company, the utility in charge of the plant, had offered to lease the unused southern half of Three Mile Island for the unbelievable price of $10 an acre.

Mayor Reed, dissatisfied with the official evacuation plan, had already drawn up plans of his own for the community. As a result 100 buses and drivers would be available on an hour's notice; printed handbills informed Middletown residents of bus locations, how to get to them, and emergency telephone numbers to use. *The Amsterdam News* reported that all 12,000 residents could be evacuated in five hours.

When, however, the Nuclear Regulatory Commission entered the scene with express authority to resolve the crisis, they supplied nothing but more chaos and confusion. Here was the Government at work.

Utility companies promote and defend the use of nuclear power plants—as does the Government. Until recently, most of the populace went along, either on the premise that nuclear power was, indeed, a necessity, or because they felt inadequate to decide pro or con. What they still don't know, says environmental writer Karl Grossman, is that the Federal bureaucracy has virtually forced nuclear power on the utilities, by threatening them with the spectre of public power should skeptics within the utilities oppose atomic energy. In short, the Government would build its own nuclear plants if the utilities didn't "play ball." To soften the blow, Congress offered some assistance. The Price-Anderson Act, for example, limits the total liability for damages, while the utilities themselves bear no direct financial obligation for radiation damage; the Federal Government, instead, standing ready to indemnify to the tune of $85 million in taxpayers' money. The balance would be forthcoming from $140 million in private insurance policy funds held by each plant, and a contribution of $5 million from each operating nuclear power station. This setup makes it far easier for utilities to get insurance for nuclear plants; without it, the plants could never be built or operated. One could not construe this as "free enterprise" by any stretch of the imagination.

The Americans of Middletown aren't the defeatist sort. They will resume their lives. But each will continue to be plagued by the question of how to preserve his community. Unfortunately, Middletown's unrest is by no means unique.

Nestled between the Cumberland Island National Seashore and Fernando Beach, on a river landing called Buttermilk Bluff, lies the town of St. Mary's, Georgia. Life there has been peaceful and easy-going—until recently. Now the installation of a Navy Fleet Ballistic Missile Squadron Port threatens the life of the tiny fishing village, which hasn't changed in a hundred years. Giant, black, Poseidon submarines will launch 68-day patrols from the new base, where nuclear-powered and armed subs are to be cleaned, re-equipped, and repaired. First, the Poseidon program will bring 5,000 Navy personnel and dependents to town. Then, with the establishment of the next generation of Trident nuclear submarines, 25,000 more military personnel will arrive at St. Mary's. There have been negative reactions from a variety of sources:

Jon Nordheimer of *The New York Times* observed: "The familiar rhythms of the pine-colored countryside have already been broken up by the introduction of a few hundred workers and sailors preparing the base."[10]

A Federal Planner, who studied the impact of the $100 million base on the area, said: "A few businessmen might prosper, but the local people usually take a beating from increased traffic congestion, crime, overcrowding of schools, and higher taxes." And from another planner: "It's strange to think that before last year very few people outside of Camden County had ever heard of St. Mary's, and now even the Russians know where St. Mary's is. I'm sure they've already targeted it."

Mayor Alvin Dickey, a craggy, Lincolnesque man, stood near a tree planted in 1799—twelve years after the founding of St. Mary's—and pondered: "We've loved to keep St. Mary's like it is, a good family town where everybody's a neighbor, where you don't need to lock your car or worry 'bout what your child is doing. But God knows things are goin' to change like we can't ever dream."

Far from St. Mary's, Crested Butte, Colorado is a "remote, enchanting setting at the end of the road in one of Colorado's last unspoiled valleys," writes Roger Neville-Williams.[11] He continues: "I was met at the plain of the North Valley by hundreds of pokey Herefords coming down the road, prodded along by mounted cowboys in snow-covered chaps—a real cattle drive. This is the old west, still mythic in its appeal, a tranquil region of range and mountains, relatively unscarred by its one compact Victorian mining town and scarcely marked by the recreation boom of the last 15 years."

Just outside Crested Butte, however, lurks a potential nightmare conjured up by AMAX, Inc. AMAX is a giant mining corporation with assets in excess of $3 billion, which wants to construct a billion-dollar molybdenum mine. Molybdenum is a metallic element noted for its resistance to corrosion and high temperatures, and is therefore invaluable in the construction of nuclear power plants. The mine site, two miles from Crested Butte, will include a mill and a tailing point (slime dump) of staggering proportions. All of this to be situated on a declared national historic site surrounded by National Forest land. Most immediately threatened is "Red Lady Mountain," the 11,000-foot Mount Emmons, as AMAX prospectors sink core drills into what they believe is the world's richest deposit of molybdenum ore.

The Town Council, led by Mayor William Mitchell, voted unanimously against the project. But they all know the harsh reality: to wit, the Mining Law of 1872 guarantees mining companies access to all mineral deposits under public lands. The local people have tried to stop the mine, and desperation has driven some to violence. A shotgun blast shattered the windows of Terry Hamlin, a local real estate agent and former head of the Ski Patrol, who is now affiliated with AMAX. Commenting on the public outrage in his town, Mayor Mitchell said: "We can't give in to the divine right of ownerhsip by mining companies. . . . What they want to do is make Gunnison County one large open pit mine." And according to Neville-Williams: "The lines are drawn in a battle that will be repeated in dozens of Crested Buttes throughout the country in the 1980's."

Unfortunately, the Government sees more and more communities as "national sacrifice areas," to be rendered up in the "national interest." Mineral exploitation, nuclear power plants, military installations, and the storing or disposal of chemical waste may all be in the Government machinery's "interest," but none is high on most citizens' lists.

Middletown, Crested Butte, St. Mary's and (of course) Love Canal once meant little or nothing to most of the country. But as the list grows, it becomes apparent that little will be left of the country after all the sacrifices are made. When all is said and done, what is the "national interest" if not the health and well-being of the communities which make up the nation?

The Black Hills Alliance, struggling to save South Dakota Indian communities from the dangers of uranium mining, stated:

> This disconnection from the land—from the meaning of the land as belonging to and *serving* a people, this loss of memory as to our place in the past and future history of our generation—we see this as the root source of the restlessness, the greed, the fragmentation which has brought us to the brink of national disaster. . . . Who speaks for the people? Who watches out for them? Whom can they trust?[12]

A new awareness does exist, and a process of resistance is developing. Increasingly suspicious of government, more and more communities are striving to decide their own fate. Endeavoring to correct the excesses of a Government which once was theirs, individuals are beginning to by-pass traditional processes. Communities have begun to assert themselves by passing laws contradicting the laws of higher legislative authorities. The Initiative and Referendum method (I & R) has been used successfully in California to reduce property taxes and to promote the adoption of rent control. Meanwhile in many parts of the country, active secessionist movements are struggling to create autonomous, self-sufficient units.

A growing desire to be freer of government control—in particular that of the Federal authority—and the burgeoning sense that traditional politics simply don't work any longer, are spurring citizens to reevaluate their society. This was eloquently expressed by the refusal of a majority of Americans to check off the $1 contribution, included on their Federal Tax Forms, to be earmarked as a national campaign kitty. Trust in government is at an all-time low. Conversely, the feeling increases that the common sense of the people may be the solution to the country's problems.

In the words of Bernard Greaves, a British social thinker:

> The movement is not a revolution, at least in the sense that is conventionally understood in politics and exemplified in the concept of the Marxist revolution, because it does not involve the total overthrow of the established political order in a single massive upheaval. It avoids the violence and bloodshed of revolution with the accompanying danger that, in the inevitable chaos which results, the objectives of the revolution will be subverted and a new authoritarian central elite seize control. Instead, it is the evolving growth of an alternative society within and along side of existing institutions which it may ultimately render, in whole or in part, redundant. Because it is a movement that is (by its nature) diffuse and diverse, it cannot be subject to central direction and it is resistant to the emergence of rigid dogmatism. Its total impact on society is likely to be more comprehensive and more deeply radical than that of any conventional political revolution, an impact that derives not from a rigid political programme nor a disciplined party, but from a new style of community politics.[13]

When Howard Jarvis launched his taxpayers' revolt, he captured the attention and the imagination of many Americans. Thomas Jefferson wrote: "Taxation without representation is tyranny." Howard Jarvis has proved that representation alone is not enough. Taxation without real accountability is also oppression.

Just as it is unresponsive to the individual's needs, the Federal system is equally ineffective in responding to the needs of communities. In most cases, it strangles on its own red tape and contradictory regulations. Agreement on this state of affairs cuts across ethnic and economic lines. Black communities oppose HUD projects in the City of New York and on Long Island for being totally ill-conceived. Meanwhile, poor, middle class and rich groups fight such "improvements" as the Westway project in New York, and the building of the World Trade Center there. These massive undertakings have so radically altered the lives of their surrounding neighbors that they have become fiercely opposed by local residents —both private and commercial.

The success of Proposition 13 bedevils public officials. Against all odds, it exemplifies the fact that people who do not hold political office *can* determine public policy. They don't have to accept either the fiats or the inaction of existing governing bodies. Concomitantly, this realization has awakened many Americans to the fact that unresponsive distant government and special interest-dominated decision making can be circumvented. They are acknowledging that communities must develop the ability to govern themselves.

What must be clearly understood is that there is no contradiction between patriotism and community autonomy, because the very concept of American democracy embodies the independence of localities. In the tiny community of DuPont, Washington, this ideal is fully understood.

Virtually everyone in DuPont owns and reveres an American flag, but the town's citizens don't accept the domination of big government. The mayor, John Iafrati, explains that the people of DuPont live by and fight for the principles of democracy and self-rule. He understands that small communities are beset by powerful and complex forces: "Why should a small community fight? Because that's our right."[14] This town boasts the lowest tax rate in the state. Its own utility runs no long-term debt and is operated by volunteer labor. The people of the town wish to control both the rate and the extent of the town's growth. Nevertheless, after consideration, they did approve the construction of a log export facility and port by the Weyerhauser Company. DuPont will, however, be participant in every phase of the environmental study and development plan. In this manner, they hope to be constructive and realistic about their economic character and the ultimate authority in their community. As Mayor Iafrati sums it up:

> Man must have freedom of choice and freedom to pursue that choice. To compromise our freedom of choice is to compromise our independence. That is something we would not do.

III. POLITICAL ACTIVITY AS A CAUSE OF EXHAUSTION

In Lawrence, New York, the proposed operation of the Concorde at nearby Kennedy Airport distressed the neighborhood. Learning of the probable noise levels of the supersonic airliner, residents organized protests effective enough to delay the Concorde's landing rights.

The power structure in the New York State Democratic Party favored landing rights for the Concorde at Kennedy but did not want to take responsibility for the consequences. Governor Carey equivocated on the issue, placing accountability on the New York Port Authority, thereby abdicating the state's responsibility.

A resident of Lawrence, Carol Berman, had been politically active in the town for many years and jumped on the Concorde controversy. She made it the basis for her candidacy for the New York State Senate. With support of the local anti-Concorde activists, she won the election—but lost the SST war. Frank Lynn of *The New York Times*, analyzing the results of the election, emphasized that although Mrs. Berman's Democratic Party credentials were well in order, it was actually the SST struggle which had brought her prominence:

> That once-heated controversy, with its auto blockades of Kennedy and stormy civic meetings, is fading with barely a whimper.
>
> The SST foes still have a suit pending in Federal Court challenging the environmental impact statement that paved the way for the Concorde to land here. But Mrs. Berman said that more money would have to be raised to pursue the court action. The civic leader turned State Senator sounded dubious about the prospects. . . .
>
> Mrs. Berman herself seemed to be reconciled to the supersonic transport. Even as a State Senator, Mrs. Berman didn't think that she could stop the SST.[15]

Perhaps it was inevitable that once elected, Mrs. Berman would say that nothing could be done at the state level. The issue had been timely and useful for her getting elected. Once installed as a freshman Senator, however, it was probably easier for her to play the game by the rules—not to make "SST-like noises." The political pattern is all too familiar.

In recent years, political experts have been bewildered by low voter turn-out for most elections. The Committee for the Study of the American Electorate recently reported that the national turn-out for the November '78 elections ebbed to the lowest level since 1942. In the gubernatorial races in New York, Connecticut, and New Jersey, the winners moved into their respective mansions with the support of roughly 25% of the eligible electorate. And not only are increasing numbers of people not voting, they are not even bothering to register. This abdication of the primary right and responsibility of American citizenship both reflects and abets an attitude of gloom. Rudell Brown of Chicago put it this way:

> I didn't even vote. Why should I help them get a job when I don't even have one? I tell you what. Look at this here mess, garbage on the side streets. It will be that way no matter who they put in City Hall.[16]

Time after time, candidates make promises, only to forget them as soon as elected. This sad state of affairs has long been a standard American political joke, but the consequences have evolved into no laughing matter. The "Vote"—that precious right—is now regarded by *the majority* of Americans as an exercise in futility. Social critic, Henry Fairlie succinctly explains that neither major political party addresses itself to the real concerns of the American citizen. Therefore, apathy is not mere indifference but the natural result of constant disappointment and betrayal.

A paralysis besets both the Democrats and the Republicans as the direct result of their sources of financial support—not because of the rosters which did or didn't vote for them. The same power brokers who have always dominated American political and legislative life finance both parties. These powerful, monied groups continually hawk the myth that every American citizen—regardless of economic station or opportunity—has the same beliefs and the same needs. Following suit, our legislators continue to operate on this erroneous premise. Thus have they lost any grasp of specific issues and real citizen requirements. Witness: Senator Robert Dole admitting to fellow Republicans who met to discuss the prospect (and avoidance) of a constitutional convention: "We've ducked the tough issues."[17] Most voters would agree.

Issue-oriented Americans have often played out a common scenario: meetings are convened; press releases produced; petitions circulated. Usually, hope and inspiration derive from a candidate-for-office who embodies the ideals and the goals of the group. Activist energy and optimism abound. Then the glorious high point, the election. Herein, victory can prove more devastating, in the long run, than defeat. For if the candidate achieves office, his constituency and concentrations diffuse.

His original sponsors may then find that the candidate's orientation shifts from the issue which got him elected to the more mundane applications of power.

Bernard Ashbell, in *The Senate Nobody Knows*, examines the process of legislative compromise and the time it takes for laws to be made. For those who struggle to elect a candidate, this process often proves grossly unproductive. An issue-oriented group deludes itself that in electoral success lies real victory. What people fail to perceive is that the function of "candidate" and "officeholder" are two very different things. For into the hoopla surrounding the victorious gladiator—weary from the battle won—enters his now-to-be constant companion; the art of compromise.

As we have seen, Carol Berman, the campaigner, fought the good fight against the SST. It must also be noted, that once elected to the New York State Senate, she was—fortuitously, it seemed—assigned to the Transportation Panel and to the State Senate Corporations and Authorities Committee. Both bodies have jurisdiction over airport legislation. Yet she chose, in her own words, to "concentrate on the economic development" of Long Island. This could be interpreted in any number of ways. It might even indicate her *support* of Concorde landing rights. In any event, it became difficult to ascertain her real position. Her campaign supporters were reduced to the option of either finding a way to pressure her to act on their behalf, or giving her up and finding another candidate to oppose her reelection. This repeated conversion from valiant warrior to circumspect "hold-the-liner" is a process which demolishes enthusiasm for the system. It disillusions and demoralizes the willing campaign worker, who then becomes reluctant ever again to commit his or her loyalties and aspirations.

On the national level, various Presidential campaigns—of winners and losers alike—have left the electorate feeling exhausted and betrayed. Since the assassination of John F. Kennedy in 1963, the Presidential campaign arena has most often evoked disappointment, if not outrage, in a citizenry which is ever-willing to concede the benefit of the doubt. Yet recent Presidential campaigns have reflected the desire for fundamental change.

The first group to address itself to the bogging down of the American system came from the Right. Conservatives perceived the overweening power of the central government and positioned themselves against increased bureaucratically dominated regulations and programs. They decried Federal arrogation of both states' and individuals' rights. They aimed to reduce the existing bureaucracy, cut taxes and, most of all, to curtail the growing power of the Presidency.

The Conservative movement coalesced in Barry Goldwater, who encouraged all who were disenchanted to support his candidacy in the 1964 Presidential election. Despite the fact that the Conservatives perceived the opposition candidate, Lyndon Johnson, as the ultimate power broker and consummate "wheeler-dealer," their energies were diverted—and sapped—by Goldwater's convention struggle against Nelson Rockefeller for the nomination. Rockefeller, a self-styled liberal, presented as divergent a posture within Goldwater's own Republican party as Johnson did from the Democratic camp. By the time the actual '64 campaign got under way, the Republican forces were riddled by schism and ill will. Johnson virtually walked into a four-year term.

As the war in Vietnam escalated, thousands of Democrats and liberals, who had merely been disenchanted, became embittered and outraged. They found a candidate in Eugene Mc-

Carthy, a soft-spoken liberal, with a politically unfortunate penchant for speaking his mind. McCarthy's candidacy was hardly noticed by the country at large, until he pulled off a *coup* in the New Hampshire Democratic Primary. Ironically, the McCarthy showing in New Hampshire convinced Robert Kennedy of the possibility of defeating the incumbent President, who was a long-time political and personal foe. Thus, Kennedy, too, threw his hat into the '68 ring. Since McCarthy and Kennedy appealed strongly to the same segments in the Democratic Party—particularly the anti-war faction—the liberal wing of the party was bitterly divided. Then came Robert Kennedy's assassination in Los Angeles and a convention marked by chaos and violence. General despair, real horror, and the experienced machinations of Chicago Mayor Richard Daley resulted in the Democrats' nominating Hubert Humphrey as their 1968 Presidential candidate.

Meanwhile, the Republicans decided to have another go with Richard Nixon. He had been edged out by John Kennedy in 1960 and assured his anxious party that he could heal the wounds left from the Goldwater-Rockefeller debacle of '64. Intriguingly—but perhaps predictably—while polls at the time showed a clear majority of Americans opposed any involvement in Southeast Asia, both Nixon and Humphrey were supportors of the war in Vietnam. Once again, Richard Nixon was involved in a close race, but this time, he won. Once ensconced in the White House, he escalated the war effort and applied various methods to quell the growing civil disobedience and anti-Administration demonstrations.

Enraged by Nixon's attitudes and policies, and desperate to end the war, activists—particularly in the Democratic Party—sought to demonstrate both verbally and concretely their disaffection from the Government. Thus, a kind of coalition formed around Senator George McGovern. His supporters consisted of a mixture of diehard McCarthy and Kennedy remnants, staunch—even fervent—anti-Nixonians, and impressionable students most of whom were too young to have been involved in '68. The rest of the country perceived McGovern supporters as radicals, but this derived more from a reflection of their anger than their ideology.

The Democratic Convention Credentials Committee was heavily stacked with Humphrey backers. The McGovern workers, whom the candidate himself had encouraged to work within the system, saw the nomination for which they had labored at the grass roots level, very nearly wrested from them on technicalities. Their momentum waned, energies dissipated, and disillusion began to take its toll.

At the convention, exciting, young, energetic workers and supporters were ridiculed by the media and taken apart by professional politicos. Beyond that, the selection of Thomas Eagleton as Vice Presidential candidate proved catastrophic. The Republicans and the media made mincemeat of McGovern over the prospect of a former mental health patient's being in the second spot on a Presidential ticket. McGovern's ill-advised attempts to stand by Eagleton further complicated the seeming "issue" and depicted him as indecisive. The election was over before it began. Richard Nixon had at long last won his coveted "landslide."

When it became impossible to continue to suppress the facts about the Nixon Administration, both during campaigns, and while in office, Vice President Agnew, then, a virtually intractable President Nixon, resigned. As a result, this electoral democracy, which serves as a model popular republic to the world, had as its top two officeholders, men who had in no way been elected to their positions: President Gerald Ford and Vice President Nelson Rockefeller. We were no longer in a position to sneer at "Banana Republic" politics.

With 1976 one would think that the major parties would welcome the chance to rectify the messes they had created—within their organizations and in the country as a whole. Instead, Ronald Reagan lost his bid for the Republican nomination, and a lackluster Gerald Ford was pitted against an unknown Georgian named Jimmy Carter. This so-called "contest" developed into the most uninformed, undistinguished Presidential campaign in memory. Televised debates were meaningless exercises, neither raising issues nor clarifying the candidates' positions. Much of the American public strongly suspected that both men were notably wanting in leadership qualities, or in any particular expertise, and that the '76 election was little more than an empty ritual in which chance was as viable a determinant as any vote count.

Thanks to the media—particularly television—the public has the growing sense that most politicians are ineffectual, ignorant or inept. Voters have begun to look elsewhere for results. One place they looked in '78 was toward Howard Jarvis and his tax reform movement. Following the 1978 elections, Richard Rovere commented in *The New Yorker*:

> The only person who played anything like a leadership role was not a politician, but an elderly entrepreneur, Howard Jarvis. The Californians who voted for his Proposition 13 were not opposing or endorsing any party or any candidate. Their cause, as they seemed to see it, was not so much political as apolitical or antipolitical—they were simply taking matters into their own hands and enacting a law themselves. . . .[18]

Voter apathy does dissipate when there is something to vote for. This was illustrated recently by the heavy turn-out in Santa Monica, California, where 80% of the voters are renters. Great numbers favored a measure known as Proposition A, which freezes rents for 190 days, then rolls them back to the levels of April, 1978. It also provides for a five-person housing board, which must approve rent increases and plans for condominium conversions. In other communities, similar rent control ordinances have been rejected—but, again, because of large voter turn-out. *What* the people decide is not as important as the fact that they finally have the chance to do so.

All too often, in this day and age, there is simply no distinction between issues or candidates—in other words, there is nothing to vote for. As Michael Palin, of Britain's satiric comedy group Monty Python, has capsulized: "We in Britain are faced with the intractable problem of all democracies—the only choice we have at an election is between politicians."[19]

In the United States, traditional party politics and Byzantine legislative processes have so sapped the faith and the vitality of citizens, that their lassitude is akin to that of Skinner's unrewarded rats. The excitement, the hope of a campaign are mere repetition, which produce neither positive results nor real action. Ring a doorbell during a campaign these days and you'll find that little or no response is forthcoming. An unmotivated organism is passive.

Human beings, however, possess the creative imagination which rats do not. They are capable of engineering new methods and systems to obtain the rewards they seek. Direct participation is one way. Community independence is another.

IV. UNHEALTHY COLLUSIONS

Mayor Maynard Jackson of Atlanta spoke to militant farmers gathered in Washington to protest the Government's agricultural policies. Wearing a farmer's cap and a grey suit, he shouted to the crowd: "I am sick and tired of being part of a system that rides to power on the backs of the masses and then turns its back on those who need it the most."[20] Jackson's attire was symbolic. The cap would seem to represent the "masses" —the gray suit, the system.

By way of circumventing pledges to the farmers, Secretary of Agriculture Bergland delineated the Government's position. He noted that the protesters had yet to present cohesive proposals for improving their lot, "and, until they do, I'm not going to respond to their individual demands."[21] Yet, acknowledging and responding to citizen demands is one of the basic tenets of a democratic system.

In his introduction to *The Regulators*, a fictional account of Shays' Rebellion, William Degenhard observed:

> . . . reading our history on a broader plane, it became apparent that civil conflicts based on the same principles recurred again and again, right down to this present day. In each case, the disaffected were soothed by palliatives that gave the illusion of dealing with the underlying issue, but in reality did not. . . .

Whatever the issue or "civil conflict" on the national scene, most Americans reject foreign ideologies based on class. Almost all Americans—even those who are not strict capitalists— support the idea of free enterprise in some form. They have been schooled in the belief that the Government exists for all the people. But it is particularly the capitalist leaders who have corrupted the American system. They have employed every segment of the Government to further their own ends —always at great expense to those without power. What's more, through their financial control of both major political parties, they have created the illusion of participatory democracy.

According to Colin Greer:

> Big government has not proved itself a worthy champion of the

various small and sundry individuals who are in fact "the public." Without doubt, government is a long way from being responsive and accountable to the public. But setting a false *private* sector in opposition to a half-hearted public sector is no more an answer than looking backwards for solutions. Indeed they are one and the same thing.[22]

As Richard Rovere pointed out, competition between the Democrats and the Republicans simply does not exist:

> ...a party system, and especially a two-party one, requires something like a parity of strength—competition enough to make victory seem a feasible goal and to give the voter a feeling that his vote matters, that there is at least a chance that his voice will be heard. It has been years since anything like real competition ... existed between our major parties.[23]

For generations, the Republican Party represented Big Business—autocratic capitalism. It told the people that business, left to its own devices, would solve all problems and, at the same time, create increased opportunity for everyone. The GOP appealed to large segments of the population, until President Hoover and the Depression. The Republicans declined in popularity, and the Democrats, bolstered by Franklin Roosevelt and Al Smith, offered a new version of democratic capitalism. They envisioned restraint and regulation in the public interest. By their lights, government direction was to promote the ideals of a democratic liberal society. Yet, for both major parties, the goal was still the same: not to allow the free enterprise system to be swallowed up, either by monopoly or by government regulation. The parties agreed that, at all costs, free enterprise must be preserved. Soon, any real party distinctions became academic. One who was critical of government interference could be a Republican; one piqued by big business, a Democrat.

In reality, government size and influence burgeon no matter which party is in power; as does the influence of industry and special interests with "connections." John Herbers, National Correspondent for *The New York Times*, has observed:

> A Republican administration, it was once believed, is good for reforming, trimming and reorganizing innovations put in place by Democrats. During the eight years of the Nixon and Ford Admin-

istrations, high officials brought in to do *something* about government traveled the country, as did the two presidents, decrying Washington bigness and interference and preaching decentralization. Yet during that period, Federal regulations took a quantum jump, and layer after layer of bureaucracy and confusion was added. . . . Mr. Carter's attempts at reforming the civil service have fared no better.[24]

It seems, then, that to wear the cap of the masses and the system's gray suit is contradictory, if not impossible. The two camps have very few interests in common and have actually grown hostile toward each other from occasions when their interests clashed.

"Winning" is important in the Democratic-Republican game. What matters is getting elected. For the victorious candidate, it means a great ego boost, with attendant feelings of personal power, and the "kick" of large favors to bestow on friends and contributors. As Senator Adlai Stevenson of Illinois mused:

> The object of a game is to win. That's what's wrong with our leadership today: their objective is not the exercise of power, but the acquisition of power.[25]

American corporations have provided the model along which the two major parties are structured and operated. A subsidiary or division of a large corporate conglomerate with diversified interests isn't free to pursue independent policies. The objectives of the parent company—however obscure—dictate policy and procedure straight through to the lowest level. For example, a company newly acquired by a holding company may even be run at a loss to serve as a tax shelter within the greater corporate structure.

A similar situation exists in the two major American political parties, particularly on the national level. The party politician seeks to rise in the organization, and to be "promoted" (elected) to higher office. His over-riding desire is to further his career, to be a good "company" man. His aims, like those of the corporate executive, include higher pay and ever greater prestige. Along the way, he finds that he is willing to sacrifice his creative ideas—or even his belief in what is right for all concerned—in order to curry favor and to gain ever-increasing sway within the organization. So goes the process of selling one's self out, supposedly in order to improve one's self. And, finally, the aggrandized, powerful "success" finds that he has bartered away every personal quality which made him unique and worthwhile.

As the politician moves through the phases of political worker, campaigner and officeholder, he or she realizes that the next level is to move from office to higher office, and so on. In order to be promoted, the candidate must be appealing enough to voters to get elected, but once those necessary games are played, the job is to attend to the people who really put him there, and will move him up: party bosses, special interests, public officials. These constitute the real Board of Directors. They will determine how far a career can go, based on their estimate of how the job is done.

Carol Bellamy, of New York, was a reformer. She advocated and practiced the idea of working within the Democratic Party to make it more open and responsibe to the needs of the people. With the backing of fellow reformers, she won a seat in the State Senate. From there she campaigned for and won the New York City Council Presidency. Ms. Bellamy's campaigns were earmarked by reformist hope and an awareness of the need for change. But when a crucial vote arose regarding the rehabilitation of Charlotte Street in the South Bronx, the reformer defected. She actually worked to defeat the plan, which involved badly needed Federal assistance for the neighborhood. In answer, a crowd of angry South Bronx residents held a mock funeral in the area proposed for urban renewal. One person hoisted a sign that read "Repent, Carol Bellamy." These were the very people who had voted for her because she had been so convincing in her desire to make things better for them.

What happened to Carol Bellamy? She wants to run for Governor—so she had better not look like a big spender. She probably still supports the project emotionally, but her career is at stake. Perhaps she sincerely believes that if she can just get elected Governor, *then* she can really do something for her constituents. But it would seem that, to date, she is taking advice from the very politicos whom she once opposed. If professional politicians help to make her Governor, would she then serve the people of the South Bronx? According to Richard Karp of *New York Magazine*, Democratic Party regulars backed her candidacy for President of the City Council. An eyewitness account gives a vivid illustration of the machinations which really do occur in the "smoke-filled-room" political world: at a meeting including, among others, David Garth, the political PR expert, and Harold Fisher, Chairman of the Metropolitan Transit Authority, Garth informed the small assembly that what Bellamy needed was a big issue—something "sexy." Incredibly, Fisher turned to Bellamy and asked: "Why don't you attack the MTA?" Then, with a perfectly straight face, he reassured the startled candidate: "I'll tell you what to say."[26]

In any event, no one person can turn the situation around. It seems for the most part that to rise in party politics one must surrender most personal ideals and beliefs. Party leadership assesses America as too conservative to accept sweeping reformism, and therefore fear that should they propose it, the country, or the district, will swing to the other party. Additionally, the party powers-that-be have accepted money from contributors whose aims and interests are anything but populist.

Every group which has sought to promote its political goals within the party structures has reaped nothing but frustration and disenchantment. Blacks are certainly familiar with this experience. More recently, the Women's Movement has discovered that party politics offers little in the way of fundamental change and is as male-dominated as any other segment of society. As is usually the case, political parties mirror the prejudices and injustice found in the greater society, often to a heightened degree, since it is these very inequities which American power interests wish to perpetuate.

In practice, Bella Abzug's ouster from an honorary position in the Carter Administration amply demonstrated this. During the '76 campaign Mrs. Abzug had worked tirelessly for Carter's candidacy and attracted much-needed feminist support. She sincerely believed, even within the context of habitual political compromise, that Carter's victory would aid in the promotion of feminist causes, particularly the success of the ERA. Her personal style has always been earmarked by candor and determination; by detractors, as over-aggressive and abrasive. Nevertheless, she is one of the tiny minority who haven't been totally undermined or co-opted by office or ambition. Her ideals and goals have remained moderately intact since her debut in the political arena: pro-community, pro-women and anti-political machines. Her personal style was not considered a detraction during the Carter campaign. In fact, her uncompromising verve won Carter votes. Why, then, was her advisory position in the Administration suddenly considered a political liability? Never once did she imply that she was unwilling to continue working within the Government in her capacity of advice and recommendation. But she implied that redress and legislation concerning women's rights were bogging down. Then, one day after President Carter had cancelled a meeting with Mrs. Abzug, it was publicly announced that she was through. She had been useful as a vote-getter, but without her wavering a jot in her tenets or goals, she became a "problem." One can only infer that she was used shamelessly by people who dropped her for continuing to display the very qualities that had made her such a campaign asset.

Time and again, spokesmen for dissenting movements are seduced into supporting a candidate or party, only to be discarded almost as soon as the victory celebration is over. Simply, they are wooed, then jilted, as officeholders return to the real business of working for their financial backers and party bosses. The lopsided courtship involves delivering up votes from movement followers and believers, who are convinced that *this time* something will really get done. It is a process of perennial betrayal.

To add insult to injury, at some levels, the major parties don't just machinate within their own houses, but actually collude, in order to dupe the public and to control the territorial spoils. This is what Judith Hope, former Appointments Secretary to Governor Hugh Carey, discovered in the course of a political career on Long Island. At one point, she was head of the East Hampton Town Democratic Committee. She found, much to her surprise, that joint meetings of Democratic and Republican Suffolk County leaders took place in the law offices of Dominic Baranello, Leader of the County Democratic Party. (Baranello later became State Chairman of the New York Democratic Committee.)

Machiavellian use of issue-oriented groups and collusion among ward and county leaders of the two parties bilk the public in an insidious and pervasive way. They more or less ensure that even with party participation by sincere and dedicated people, the "best and the brightest" will be co-opted, subverted or eventually, shut out.

Republicans, like Ronald Reagan, make fiscally conservative noises, but at the same time receive backing from interests which expect to have the continued benefits of the existing system. They may be contractors with heavy public works dealings, or suppliers of military hardware, or businesses with money at stake in Taiwan or Panama. Perhaps this is the reason that Republicans are leading the fight against a constitutional convention for an Amendment requiring a balanced national budget.

The Democrats, meanwhile, continue to try to be all things to all people—from big labor to big business. There is California Governor Jerry Brown for the budget balancers; Ted Kennedy for what is left of the "Left;" Carter for the moderates.

It was eloquently symbolic that, during the '79 farmers' demonstration in Washington, the police blocked off all the avenues, and the farmers had to drive their tractors in circles. That is, indeed, what happens to any group wishing to promote an issue or express a grievance. The Government bulwarked by the two parties, closes off the system, blocks off all avenues of protest. The result: petitioners end up going in circles. The farmers were so incensed that they destroyed their own tractors, burning some, driving others into a reflecting pool. With the rest, they began churning up the earth. This is the kind of disillusion and anger which the system engenders; emotions which at last turn back on themselves in despair and self-destruction. Because the Government stifles any real expression of grievance or criticism, feelings are subverted into hatred and squandered. American history bears numerous eloquent testimonials to this process, and it must be stopped. If nothing else, the political parties should be arenas for promoting action and ideas. But they are so corrupted by prostitution to their backers and personal lust for power, that they are incapable of addressing any of the real problems in our society.

Thus, without a true forum for debate, voters often cannot even delineate the issues—let alone decide upon them. Methods for reform or change are never components of the electoral process. When desperation in the form of violent protest erupts, it is characterized as the irrationality of a fringe group or small minority. Loathing domestic violence, the majority of Americans have no recourse but to passively endure existing policy, since attempts to accomplish change within the system will almost always be subverted or rendered into nothingness. Nevertheless, dissatisfaction prevails—currently, without a constructive or viable outlet.

If, indeed, both the two-party system and the over-all governmental structure are obsolete and ineffective, constructive change will come about only when they are by-passed. That is one reason for the movement toward direct democracy through I & R and increased demand for community autonomy. Very simply, these are faster, more efficient and more productive ways to get things done. They also offer much more readily accessible information and issue delineation to the voter than does a media-antiseptic candidate. Arthur Schlesinger, Jr., writing of the decline of the political party, blames television and computerized public opinion polls for its slide. According to Tom Wicker, these technological developments, "tend to make the national political party as obsolete as the gas-guzzler."[27]

NOTES TO PART ONE

1. New York Times, May 6, 1979, Long Island Section.
2. New York Times Magazine, April 22, 1978.
3. New York Times, April 17, 1979.
4. New York Times, 1979.
5. New York Times, February 24, 1979 A8.
6. New York Times, April 17, 1979 A 19.
7. Geekie, *Why Government Fails,* Libra Publishers, Roslyn Heights, N.Y., 1976.
8. New York Times, April 22, 1979.
9. New York Times, 1979.
10. New York Times, March 20, 1979.
11. New York Times Magazine, March 4, 1979.
12. Smoke Signals, Vol. No. 5, May, 1979.
13. "Communities and Power" in *Community Politics,* Peter Hain, ed., John Calder, (Publishers) London 1976.
14. New York Times, July 4, 1979.
15. New York Times, 1979.
16. New York Times, 1979.
17. New York Times, February 5, 1979.
18. *The New Yorker,* November 9, 1978.
19. New York Times, April 27, 1979.
20. New York Times, February 7, 1979.
21. Ibid.
22. New York Times, April 16, 1979.
23. *The New Yorker,* November 9, 1978.
24. New York Times Magazine, April 22, 1979.
25. New York Times, February 9, 1979.
26. Copyright 1979 by News Group Publications, Inc. Reprinted with the permission of *New York Magazine,* April 9, 1979.
27. New York Times, 1979.

PART TWO

THE COURSE

V. WORLD-WIDE FEVER

Once, in Gojam, a remote province of Ethiopia, a young man who wanted to show me the region, took me to an island on Lake Tana. We passed through dense rain forest, until we reached a clearing. There stood one of the area's noted Coptic churches, constructed of chika, or dried mud, with a thatched roof.

A large crowd of people had assembled. A priest was addressing the gathering, and my guide interpreted. The gist of the meeting was that the people—traditional Africans, of all ages—resented paying taxes to support the government in Addis Adaba. Their money was being spent on fancy buildings, which, as far as they were concerned, had no use. I laughed, and my young companion grew angry: "Why are you laughing at these people?" I explained that I was in no way deriding them. Rather, the situation reminded me vividly of the U.S. He responded with a smile of understanding; citizens everywhere have the same problems. All central governments, whether run by emperors, presidents, prime ministers, or for that matter, revolutionary councils, want to augment their power—usually at the expense of the general population.

Espousing "thinking small," Leopold Kohr, Professor of Political Philosophy at the University of Wales, has authored *The Breaking Down of Nations.* Of government's perpetual aggrandizement, he says:

> Measuring their greatness by the size of the institutions over which they preside, politicians have a vested interest in enlarging, not reducing, their principalities. Even if they consider it good public relations to concede to a rising number of hecklers that there may be beauty in smallness, they rarely fail to add that, progress being what it is, it makes no sense to step back. To this argument, the Welsh anthropologist, Alwyn Rees, used to remark, "When you have reached the edge of the abyss, the only thing that makes sense is to step back."[1]

All around the globe, movements to reduce the size and power of centralized government have gotten underway. A lot has been written on the subject of how institutions have outgrown their viability and their usefulness. Citizens of many countries feel themselves alienated, but still ill-used, by self-generative, monolithic bureaucracies. Though wholly unresponsive to individuals, these forces still manage to impinge upon every facet of individual life. The people of many national communities perceive the monster of immensity and over-centralization and want to draw things back into the realm of manageability. The process of slaying the dragon is, however, not easy, as Professor Kohr points out:

> ... it is not war, poverty or unemployment that threatens our survival—they are to history what dryness is to the desert or moisture is to the sea. What should concern us vitally is *big war, massive poverty, huge unemployment rates*. What threatens the life of modern society is not the nature but the scale of the problems. ... A return to manageable small political units as a solution to the intractable problems of bigness thus may be regarded as considerably more realistic than is conventionally assumed. The real obstacle is not practical, but mental, summed up in that mind-arresting slogan of the politicians that you cannot turn back the clock. *They* probably cannot. But most of us do this with the greatest of ease whenever our timepiece runs faster than time.[2]

Much of Kohr's argument draws upon the economics of E.F. Schumacher, whose *Small Is Beautiful* outlines a global approach to smallness as the basic solution to human problems. Along the same lines, Andre Bercoff, former cultural editor of *L'Express,* proposes:

> ... the strengthening of civil society and direct democracy; the recovery of each citizen's control over his own life free of a state that has for too long been super-centralized ... The time has come for it to divest itself of some of its powers ... there must be real decentralization, the establishment of regional and departmental assemblies elected by universal suffrage and the transfer of direct income taxation to these local collectives, since real decision-making power demands the financial means that make it effective. ...[3]

These opinions seem increasingly universal, reflecting the populist unrest across the globe. Forces within Britain and France are agitating for autonomy and self-determination: Brittany and Corsica in France; Scotland, Wales and Northern Ireland in Britain. Even tiny Cornwall has raised the question of its ancient right of home rule. A homogeneous territory, or a community of people, absorbed by a larger entity suffers a tremendous sense of loss—of control, of culture, of identity. Jan Morris, speaking of Wales:

> It is a conquered nation, annexed forcibly to the English crown; and hard although it is for the unconquerable English to imagine it, the neurosis of defeat, compounding resentment with convictions of inadequacy, have lingered in Wales since the terrible castles of the English domination arose beyond the mountains in the 13th Century. [4]

With the exception of Ulster, the Irish have never permitted England to dominate them and have fought for hundreds of years until they gained full independence as a nation. The results have been astounding. Long regarded as a poverty-stricken people, dependent on Britain for survival, the Irish fled to the United States, Canada and Australia for independence and prosperity. Now, the Irish economy is booming, while Britain's stagnates. Irish independence is in no way the disaster predicted. Indeed, it has proved an unqualified success.

Scotland's current situation would likely be reversed, if the Scots had control of their own natural wealth, especially the off-shore oil in the North Sea. As a matter of fact, eleven Scottish Nationalist Members of Parliament were largely responsible for bringing down the Callaghan Labor Government, because it did not support their cause satisfactorily.

In Spain, a new constitution acknowledges some autonomy for the regions which have long sought it—most particularly, the Basque provinces and Catalonia. What's more, the citizens of these regions have elected nationalist majorities to their city councils and are pressing for a municipal act to further empower local governments. Eventually, Catalans hope to establish their language on an equal basis with Spanish and by assuming more authority over the distribution of taxes, to control education, industrial relations and agricultural policy. The Basques go even further—they want to establish their own nation.

The Belgians have altered their constitution to alleviate ethnic and linguistic strife, by dividing the country into two federated states: the northern, Flemish; the southern, French. Brussels will become a separate bilingual district called Cloobia.

The same sort of solution may have to be adopted in Cyprus, where Greeks and Turks have battled for ages; in Lebanon, where one region has already broken away; and in Yugoslavia, where a resurgence of Croatian nationalism threatens Eastern European stability. Meanwhile, the Palestinians continually struggle for autonomy on the West Bank and in Gaza; their deplorably violent behavior, the result of decades of occupation. In fact, some leading Israeli intellectuals have suggested that Palestine might secede unilaterally from an enlarged Israel to effect independence.

Even in South and Central America, Indian populations express resentment of the domination by Iberian culture, and claim there is no such entity as "Latin" America. The name was, in fact, coined by a French civil servant to suit his own linguistic and cultural characterization of the area. It was through conquest that Spanish and Portuguese control and culture were imposed; they were not willingly adopted.

In Sri Lanka, the Tamils are attempting to restore the Hindu kingdom which flourished 2,000 years ago. One Tamili-speaking Jaffna grocer declares: "They don't want Tamils down in the rest of the country, and we don't want Sinhalese up here. Why not make two countries out of the place and be done with it?" [5]

Chad's southern provinces are currently torn. Bangladesh has already broken away from Pakistan and formed a new country. In India, Naga tribesmen and the Sikhs persist in their fight for freedom.

Ethiopia is riddled with separatist movements. Despite a government effort to suppress them—aided by Cuban troops and Soviet arms and advisors—the secessionists will not yield. Secessionist struggles have divided many African countries. Two notable examples: Zaire, when it was the Congo, and Nigeria, scene of the Biafran struggle. Currently, in Northern Africa, the Polisario's battle both Morocco and Mauritania for self-determination.

In fact, in much of the Third World, recent nationalistic revolutions and wars for independence haven't encompassed the demands for autonomy from smaller sectors. In Indonesia, the South Mallucans demand their own country and are terrorizing Holland for not assisting them. Indonesian East Timor continues to resist forced annexation, at a cost of the lives of one-sixth of the population thus far, with more projected. Anthropologist Shepard Forman calls this "the annihilation of a simple mountain people."[6] Of this struggle, Eqbal Ahman has said:

> The hope for a timely and just peace lies in public opinions induc-
> ing Western governments, especially the United States Govern-
> ment, to withhold arms supplies until Indonesia heeds the United
> Nations' call for the exercise by Timoris of the right of self-
> determination.[7]

In Iran, the Ayatollah Hosseini, who represents the long-oppressed Kurds, has asserted that the revolution for them is not over:

> We fought in the revolution not out of religious conviction, but
> for political reasons. We want autonomy—our own parliament,
> our own language, our own culture. The revolution has destroyed
> despotism, but it has not ended discrimination against minorities.
> The revolution must go on until all major minority groups . . . win
> a measure of autonomy. Iran is a big country and can be fed-
> erated like other big countries.[8]

Even the ostensibly monolithic Communist block is not exempt from its own versions of this world-wide foment. Zviad Gramsakhurdia, a dissident native of Soviet Georgia, has described his homeland republic as "maybe half-independent already. Maybe it is possible to be in the Soviet Union formally but in fact, be independent. . . . Why must the Russians swallow other people? They have them in their stomach, but they are not yet digested." [9] Through demonstrations alone, undaunted university students had Georgian restored as the first language of the republic. Ironically, this is all very much in keeping with Marxist doctrine. A "withering away of the state" would lead to a Europe of autonomous, ethnic communities, similar to those of the Middle Ages. Originally, Lenin acknowledged the right of secession in the creation of the Soviet Union; at one point, the Soviet Constitution even encompassed that right. Stalin, however, undermined this, encouraging total domination by the central government. Of course, this led to fewer and fewer rights in the hands of the republics.

In China, too, the swallowing of a people has led to acute indigestion. Speaking for Tibet, the Dalai Lama has said:

> ... the nature of our struggle is not anti-Communist, anti-reform or even anti-Chinese. It is also not whether those of us in exile can return to Tibet. Fundamentally, the real issue is the happiness and welfare of the six million Tibetans inside Tibet. We are carrying out our freedom movements in accordance with the wishes of the people there. The majority of them, especially the young, are not at all happy with the Chinese and are not willing to live under their domination. . . . Why should alien rule be forced upon six million people? Why shouldn't they be given the right to choose for themselves? [10]

As we very well know, North America is no more immune than the rest of the world to the fever of self-determination. In perhaps the only true example of full-blown secession, Quebec is trying to break away from Canada. Rene Levesque, long the leading spokesman for the province's separatist movement, believes the degree of autonomy necessary depends on the particular situation in each country. For his own homeland, he stresses the importance of the French language as a source of cultural independence:

> We have taken rational measures—we think they are civilized measures—to insure normal promotion of our language. We are a community that does not intend to go down the drain. [11]

In an interview with William Stockton, in *The New York Times* "Magazine," Levesque summarized his separatist philosophy, in conjunction with a federated-type association:

> A relatively small North American community like Quebec will never be healthy if it doesn't have this chance of maturity which goes with being responsible. It doesn't mean waving a flag and shouting nationalistic slogans. But, if you're responsible for yourself as a people, then you can't blame other people if things go wrong. Basically, if you're responsible for your own development and ordering your own society, then you move forward. [12]

In the United States, Levesque's objectives are of no small interest and concern. William Safire has written: "I see him as modern Jeff Davis with this difference; Levesque is likely to win. No stubborn Abe Lincoln sits in Ottawa with an oath registered in Heaven to preserve the Union."[13] But, if Levesque's goals seem far-fetched and threatening to Americans because of the obvious analogy to our Civil War, those Canadians who oppose secession regard them as untenable, even horrifying.

A government commission, The Task Force on Canada Unity, reports that the country is in "a crisis of existence," and urges that the federal and provincial governments restructure political institutions to accommodate not only Quebec, but any other dissatisfied regions, too. The Commission upholds the right of self-determination—even separatism—for Quebec, and opposed any use of force to thwart that aim. The report determines:

> . . . the pressing need today is to discover the basis for a fresh accommodation which will permit the people who inhabit this vexing and marvelous country to live together in peace, harmony and liberty.

Even Prime Minister Pierre Trudeau realizes that, in order for a federal system to survive, it must respond to demands for greater local control. But the Commission report, going further, noted:

> If in the course of the next few years, Quebec decided definitely and democratically to secede, ought that decision to be respected and accepted by the rest of Canada? To that question, we answer an unequivocal yes. Our response is a virtual corollary of our acceptance of the democratic process.

To prevent Quebec's breaking away, Ottawa could concede principles of regionalism and a share of governing responsibility. The report concludes: "Quebec is distinctive and should, within a viable Canada, have the powers necessary to protect and develop its distinctive character." To achieve this end in the country as a whole, the Commission suggests each province be given an equally augmented degree of autonomy, which could be delegated back to the Federal Government.

This concurrent international phenomenon, the breaking down of nations, involves much more than the question of ethnic identity. In part, it pertains to the quality of life in a demonically centralized, economically-oriented system. For instance, introduction of technological schemes has produced geometric increases of hypertension in formerly "backward" peoples. Their governments convince them they must have all the modern "conveniences," including the latest forms of transportation. Yet, the increased pressure and speed inherent in "being civilized" are the very roots of a pronounced dilemma. Professor Kohr suggests that velocity and human progress do *not* go hand-in-hand. In fact, the hard correlation between speed and cultural advancement directly opposes the betterment of life:

> ... national populations can be reduced to manageable proportions not by reducing their numbers but simply by slowing down their pace. It is our increasingly motorized existence that, compounded by political integration, causes people to live at ever greater distances, requiring ever faster speeds to reconnect what progress has flung apart. Hence to decelerate their pace, it is not enough to tell them to slow down as an alternative to extermination. What must be done is to recreate a compact and roughly self-sufficient environment of units so that high speeds are no longer necessary in the first place.

> ... At the national level, deceleration can be brought about by cantonizing the regions, giving the remoter areas of a state full-fledged governments able to take care of their own affairs. With more autonomy in planning and administration, each region can provide sufficient convivial, economic and political resources to satisfy its citizens.... [14]

Thus, the revolt against the tyranny of technology and the concomitant monolithic state, stems from an instinct for self-preservation. People the world over are beginning to realize that technical "progress" may not be so good for individuals and communities after all. Worse than increased health problems, technology can pose actual life threats: faster (and ever more shoddily produced) automobiles and airplanes are legion; industrial effluvia is rampant. Today, however, the most gruesome threat is posed by the government-encouraged tinkering with nuclear energy. In Switzerland a referendum passed approving the development of nuclear energy. Now the Swiss are having second thoughts. The Austrians, on the other hand, used the referendum method to oppose the construction of even one plant. The American people have never had the issue submitted to them for a vote. Rather, the Governmental machine rumbles on, serving its own interests in the name of "technology," without consideration to the desires—even the well-being—of its citizenry.

Even with the area of technology itself, community autonomy would again seem to be appropriate. The pros and cons of a given question or application should be decided by the people who will be primarily affected. They are the ones who should balance employment and economic benefits against potential dangers. In the matter of nuclear power plants, certainly, it should be up to the public whether or not to accept so volatile a bedfellow.

We must consider, as Terry Sanford once advised the City of New York, going on a diet under the strict supervision of a physician: the diet, to diminish our size for better health; the physician, the people. The Government is a compulsion which, if left to its own devices, will persist in its deadly addiction to rampant growth.

VI. AMERICAN CASE HISTORIES

In 1848, Frenchman Alexis de Tocqueville, described this country's political life in his classic work, *Democracy in America:*[15]

> In the township, as well as everywhere else, the people are the source of power; but nowhere do they exercise their power more immediately. In America the people form a master who must be obeyed to the utmost limits of possibility.

There were no costly legislative bodies, no salaried assemblymen or congressmen, nor were there any standing, automatic taxes:

> [Here] where the legislative and administrative action of the government is nearer to the governed, the system of representation is not adopted. There is no municipal council; but the body of voters, after having chosen its magistrates, directs them in everything that exceeds the simple and ordinary execution of the laws of the state. . . .
>
> . . . In all affairs that are voted in town meetings . . . the selectmen carry into effect the popular mandate . . . If, for instance, a school is to be established, the selectmen call a meeting of the voters on a certain day at an appointed place. They explain the urgency of the case; they make known the means of satisfying it, the probable expense, and the site that seems to be most favorable. The meeting is consulted on these several points; it adopts the principle, marks out the site, votes the tax, and confides the execution of its resolution to the selectmen. . . .
>
> . . . The selectmen alone have the right of calling a town meeting; but they may be required to do so. If ten citizens wish to submit a new project to the assent of the town, they may demand a town meeting; the selectmen are obliged to comply and have only the right of presiding at the meeting.

All town functions were the responsibility of all the people, including taking care of the poor. As for the performance of public duty:

> In general, each official act has its price, and the officers are remunerated in proportion to what they have done.

The townships were, at this time, independent and separate. Of the relationship of these communities to the nation, de Tocqueville ascertained that:

> ...political life had its origins in the townships: and it may almost be said that each of them originally formed an independent nation ... They did not receive their power from the central authority, but, on the contrary, they gave up a portion of their independence to the state ... not a man is to be found who would acknowledge that the state has any right to interfere in town affairs.

In the Frenchman's estimation, love of country stemmed from the citizen's freedom to govern himself through community independence and real democracy:

> The township of New England possesses two advantages which strongly excite the interest of mankind: namely, independence and authority ... The New Englander is attached to his township ... because it is a free and strong community, of which he is a member, and which deserves the care spent in managing it. The American attaches himself to his little community for the same reason that the mountaineer clings to his hills, because the characteristic features of his country are there more distinctly marked; it has a more striking physiognomy.

> ... The native of New England is attached to his township because it is independent and free; his cooperation in its affairs ensures his attachment to its interests; the well-being it affords him secures his affection; and its welfare is the aim of his ambition and of his future exertions. He takes a part in every occurrence in the place ... he accustoms himself to those forms without which liberty can only advance by revolutions ... and collects clear practical notions on the nature of his duties and the extent of his rights.

This was America's past: small, independent mini-republics, where citizen control devolved from a system of direct democracy. Only a handful of people comprised the state government, with its few administrative functions. Those of advanced age and experience presided over a limited Federal Government, concerned mainly with international relations. And only the more involved and talented individuals devoted themselves to the life of their communities.

Everett Rattray, in his study of eastern Long Island, THE SOUTH FORK, confirms de Tocqueville's theses. Of East Hampton, he concludes that:

> ...like most of its fellow towns on Long Island, it was established as an independent republic in embryo—an offspring of the Massachusetts Bay Colony—long before there was a United States.... The East End towns of Long Island still dream of the days when they were on their own, looked to New England only for advice, and to Manhattan, Dutch or English, for little but trouble... 16

This sense of freedom is still at issue, as shown by a news item in *The Southampton Press*. To parry state efforts to break Southampton's exclusive freshwater fishing rights, Town Trustee President Rewinski promised resistance. He cited the 1688 Dongan Patent which provides " . . . the Trustees authority to regulate any activities in town waters."

> "The waters of this town are privately owned by the people of Southampton," said Mr. Rewinski. "They (state officials) think they are a higher authority, but we think we are. We were here before the state and before the federal government." Under the Dongan Patent, authority over all waters in the town "as long as water flows and grass grows" was given to the town by the English king.17

The early American settlers shared a spirit of independence with the Indians. Those original Americans lived in separate, sovereign nations. They were self-sufficient and resided in harmony with nature. Their many survival skills, freely imparted, chiefly enabled the European newcomers to get through their first years on this continent. Perhaps the hard reality that survival depended directly on self-sufficiency aided in the creation of the independent community. What's more, during this period, amenable relations existed between the settlements and the Indian nations. Mutual respect deteriorated only with the onset of the Europeans' drive to expand and to dominate.

Initially, commerce among the colonies didn't erode that spirit of local independence. Business relations were not government-regulated, but individually negotiated and conducted. Common sense and cooperation dictated "public interest." Because each citizen had a vested interest in the common good, government restraint was not only unnecessary, it was unthinkable. Agricultural, commercial and civic duties were shared for the sake of the community and for the betterment of the individual.

As de Tocqueville so astutely ascertained, the American Revolution was fought not only for independence from England, but for the right of self-determination; and thus was the first expression of American distaste for any distant, centralized authority.

The Constitution was the vehicle for reconciling individual and community freedoms with the need for some central authority. Jefferson warned against excessive centralization as it was sought by Hamilton and the Federalists. For Jefferson, such a system was inherently dangerous, both in the private and public sectors, as it would eventually impinge upon individual rights and dignity. He perceived that local government, being closest to the people is the most accessible and effective. Although Jefferson probably represented the more widespread feelings of the general populace, his ideas were altered in the hands of the hard-nosed men of commerce, who were not concerned with democracy or freedom, but with their own financial gains.

As the community expanded and government became more focalized, communities were seduced into conceding more and more of their powers. Political party affiliation began to supersede community attachment and, gradually, bureaucracy usurped more and more citizen responsibility.

As these processes unfurled, a few idealistic Americans sought to preserve pure democracy by establishing small Utopian groups, which were almost totally independent—both politically and economically. Usually established apart from other centers of population, these settlements were designed along communal lines, with residents supplying all community needs. Such groups were fully autonomous in conducting their affairs, and citizens turned to other members of the collective for help. Many settlements—most notably the Shakers—excelled in agriculture and various forms of craftsmanship, with enlightened and progressive applications of new technologies. Communities similar to the Shaker Village sprang up at Oneida, New York; New Harmony, Indiana; and Brentwood, Long Island, among other places. Interestingly, so successful were some of these experiments that Engels believed they constituted an argument for the practicability of communism. Charles Norhoff, analyzing this contention in 1875 in THE COMMUNIST SOCIETIES OF THE UNITED STATES found:

> ...it is true that a commune, to exist harmoniously, must be composed of persons who are of one mind upon some question which to them shall appear to take the place of religion, if it is not essentially religious, though it need not be fanatically held.[18]

From the American vantage point, it is most important that Utopian communities were established not with a view to overthrowing the established order, but to recapturing an essential spirit lost in the country's expansion. This desire for "going back" has pervaded American dissension and reformist thinking over the years. Author David De Leon proffers that:

> This indigenous radicalism is rooted in our history and assumes that however much this society may be changed or transformed, it is unlikely to become *wholly* dissimilar from what it has been. It is radical then in the sense that it seeks a complete realization of the democratic potential that it perceives within our past.[19]

Even today, travelling in the rolling countryside of Pennsylvania, one sees the pristine farms and grazing cows of the Amish settlements. These are a pacific people, who, being virtually self-sufficient in supplying their own material needs, have rejected most of the products of modern industrial technology. They band together in communities governed directly and eschew all forms of state interference in their affairs. Yet, they do not consider themselves apart from America; they believe that they are the *real* America.

The traditions of the small town and the congeniality of the compact community are celebrated in American literature and drama and rendered with clarity and love in its artwork. American nostalgia for smallness and closeness—for life on a human scale—is overwhelming. The "town" and the Utopias represent a longed-for part of our past. Whether misused by the Government-industrial complex, or ridiculed as naive by scoffers, or recreated as a fantasy in Disneyland, it is presented to us as a fiction, in which we may not dwell. Yet, the distance we have travelled from Jefferson's vision has exacted a terrible price. Bigness and bureaucracy have actually become obstacles to our real advancement—perhaps even threats to our very survival. Faceless government functionaries and ambitious corporate executives instruct us to look forward for the solutions to our manifold problems. Rather, it would seem that a good look backward might provide us better models with which to work.

VII. RADICAL-CONSERVATIVE STIRRINGS

America is not alone in realizing that we must look to our origins for solutions to current problems. However, because Americans often aren't as historically-oriented as other nationals, they are not always fully aware that looking backwards is just what they're doing. For instance, opposition to the war in Vietnam was regarded by many as a radical endeavor. Yet, from George Washington's farewell address, in which he warned against "foreign entanglements," rises a foreshadowing of that dissension. A balanced national budget, considered by many to be the *cause celebre* of today's conservatives, inflamed our forefathers with equal passion. Jefferson, the leading liberal of his day, was most outspoken on this issue:

> There does not exist an engine so corrupt of the government and so demoralizing of the nation as public debt. It will bring on us more ruin at home than all the enemies from abroad against whom the army and navy are to protect.

As Lowell Ponte has pointed out:

> . . . Jefferson favored the rural over the urban, farm over factory, decentralization of power over centralization. On balance, Jefferson's sympathies lay with the centrifugal, not the centripetal forces in our new nation.[20]

Today, Stephen Gaskin, a product of the San Francisco "hippy" movement, is probably considered radical by many Americans. He characterizes himself as apolitical, summing it up in two words: "Govern yourself."[21] Gaskin founded and heads The Farm, a 1,750-acre community in Tennessee, where some 1,200 people live. In a rustic setting, the collective grows all its own food organically, has its own free laundromat, its own telephone system, and even, its own health care system. The Farm operates as a non-profit corporation, which as Gaskin explains: " . . . was the closest thing available to seceding from the Union."[22]

Self-government and sufficiency are the bases for a way of life which reveres life, a style of existence in which *people* are the number-one priority. In an independent situation, like

The Farm, individuals not only can control their own lives, but can cooperate for the good of the whole as well. Stephen Gaskin's views correspond with those of California's Jerry Brown. Gaskin has said:

> ...in order to lower the government spending, what you have to do is to get up from in front of your television set and go out in the street and take care of somebody who needs to be taken care of so it doesn't have to be done by the government.[23]

Conversely, Gaskin also identifies with Barry Goldwater:

> ...I fight for the standards. Fighting for the standards makes me understand Barry Goldwater. That's all he was really doing; he was fighting for what he figured were the standards.[24]

A former speechwriter for Goldwater, Karl Hess is considered an archetypical conservative, who advises neglected communities to "rise up;" to "secede."[25] Coming from the totally opposite side of the political coin, Tom Hayden, one of the founders of SDS, has expressed similar sentiments:

> The emphasis in the movement on "letting people decide," on decentralized decision-making, on refusing alliances with top leaders stems from the need to create a personal and group identity that can survive both the temptations and the crippling effects of this society.[26]

Long Island, New York, that seemingly dangling geographic extension of the state, has long been neglected by the state government in Albany. Regarded by many up-staters as an appendage of New York City, it has always been subject to very heavy taxation. Now, as local citizen groups rally for redress and reform, it is the scene of a tax rebellion and several secessionist movements.

Once a rural and coastal paradise, Long Island farmlands were rich and extensive; the coastal marshlands teemed with variegated sea and bird life. Miles and miles of unspoiled white sand beaches ringed the area. Then, the State of New York bulldozed highway after highway up and down the island. With speedier access to and egress from New York City, Nassau County (bordering the city's borough of Queens) has become totally suburbanized, and the easternmost county, Suffolk, is heading in the same direction. The subsequent overcrowding has spawned only quick solutions to provide adequate community services, with predictable miscalculation.

Today, the special interests dominate the area and its politicians are pressing for even more highways, a bridge across Long Island Sound and nuclear power plants for the area. The giant $1 billion Southwest Sewer District will pump vast quantities of effluent into the ocean, thus threatening the survival of the clamming industry in Great South Bay. Federally-funded Brookhaven reactor, which has made the Peconic River dangerously radioactive menaces a once-thriving fishing industry. The nuclear reactor at Shoreham—a bucolic North Shore community—is scheduled to be operative within two years. Surrounded by gentle fields and hauntingly beautiful wetlands, Shoreham has looked out on the Sound for hundreds of years. Now, dominating the landscape, stands the ominous eyesore of a nuclear power plant. Two more nuclear plants were planned for Jamesport, a tiny farming community.

Meanwhile, the Long Island Expressway, a six-lane swath from one end of Long Island to the other, is in marked disrepair, while the Department of Transportation diverts most of its $270 million in Federal funds from Expressway improvement to other uses in metropolitan New York. Depending on one's perspective, the Long Island Railroad, under aegis of the Metropolitan Transit Authority (MTA), has long been a commuter joke or tragedy. Yet the state refuses to allocate the funds necessary to improve, or even properly maintain it. When one enterprising young entrepreneur started a jitney line to and from New York, he provided a much-needed service. But when he applied to the state for permission to run a larger bus, the MTA opposed it on the grounds that he was competing with the Long Island Railroad.

For these, and many other reasons, *Newsday* reported that fifty Long Island businessmen have launched a campaign to declare Long Island the 51st state. Said Arthur Chadwick of Statehood for Long Island, Inc.:

> We are average people, no celebrities, no superstars . . . We're based at Post Office Box 500, Wheatley Heights, Long Island 11798. Don't use "New York" in the address.

These separatist-oriented businessmen realize that rapid and unplanned growth amply benefits the few insiders, while the mass of people find themselves in overcrowded, over-taxed, under-serviced and heavily polluted communities. Moreover, the high cost of electricity and the acute rate of taxation are driving away many of the businesses once located in the area. This, of course, paints a still gloomier picture of taxation to come.

In the Hamptons, the most remote easterly part of Suffolk County, a more radical group has proposed the creation of a new nation on Long Island's South Fork. Their petition for secession listed well known grievances: destruction of the local environment, inflation, high taxes, unemployment, the declining quality of public education. Technically, the South Fork stands as a separate island, with a canal between it and the main body of Long Island. Thus, the idea was to join in a federation with Martha's Vineyard, Nantucket, Block Island and Fisher's Island. Begun virtually in jest, the movement gained momentum and support, and, with the onset of serious press coverage, early members of the group began to wonder what they had wrought.

The separatists invited the five eastern Long Island towns to join the movement, and while they did not accept the idea of separate nationhood, the concept of secession from Suffolk County, to form Peconic County, was revived.

As with Proposition 13 in California, real estate taxes on Long Island are a prevalent issue. Former Suffolk County Legislator Martin Feldman of Huntington has proposed an increase in the tax rate on undeveloped land. This would benefit the overly developed and more populous West End of Suffolk, but would severely burden eastern Long Island landowners, many of whom are farmers. According to Ed Sharretts, an active member of the Peconic County movement, by breaking away, the East End could avoid footing all the bills for county projects which benefit only the West End.:

> ... the East End is primarily agricultural and resort, the West End industrial and residential. The two things don't mix well. The West End tries to use us, not help us. Every day the need for Peconic County gets greater.[27]

Birthed by a radical-conservative union of irate and independent citizens, the separatist Peconic County movement was given an additional spur when Western Suffolk lawmakers decided to force East Enders to pay taxes into the Suffolk County Police District, despite the fact that, some years ago, the five towns had voted overwhelmingly to reject being included in the district. Instead, they retained their own local departments, financing them with town revenues. The proponents of their continued inclusion in the district sought more revenue at the county level in order to supply salary hikes to police officers serving in the West End—officers who, according to *The Southampton Press*, were already among the highest paid in the nation.

Eschewing such misdirection of their monies, civic leaders favoring Peconic County want more accessible, local governance on all levels. Evans Griffing, the former supervisor of the Town of Shelter Island, elucidates:

> Peconic County would elect officials from its own environment who would have a feeling for its environment . . . The people who are ultimately elected to govern Peconic County will be residents . . . and they will selfishly want to protect what we've got.

> The people of eastern Suffolk are more self-employed, more small businessmen, and working for themselves than the people numerically in the western County. We have a great deal more independence and self-dependence out East than they have at the West End. Many people on the West End, the vast majority of them, are simply employees of corporations. They don't have to make decisions that are vital to their very existence. Out East, agriculture and small businessmen have to make decisions to determine whether they're going to survive or not. And that has a tendency to make every individual more self-reliant in the long run. And I feel that we have the beginning or the nucleus of a very decent, fundamental county of the five eastern towns, because of the simple independence of the individual.[28]

In the East End communities it is still possible to survive by farming, fishing and clamming. In the face of encroaching big business and urban sprawl from Metropolitan New York and western Long Island, Griffing sees only one possibility for the area's preservation: independence and local autonomy.

To prove the idea can work, a municipal accountant has

been retained to do a cost analysis of Peconic County. Meanwhile, each of the five towns has apppointed a representative to a committee in favor of Peconic. State Assemblyman John Behan of Montauk has introduced a Bill to the State Legislature providing for separation of the East End from Suffolk County and the establishment of the new County.

As the Peconic movement picks up steam, I think of a friend of mine, who, tired of Suffolk County politics, fled to Ibiza, Spain, After he left, *The New York Times* reported:

> . . . a revival of sentiment in favor of Ibizan autonomy . . . The island's only newspaper, the conservative *Diaro de Ibiza*, formerly favored Francoist centralism but now advocates autonomy, in which the great foe is the largest of the Balearics, Majorca. "To get anything done, to get a driver's license, or any kind of permit, you have to go to Majorca," said Nestor Torres . . . [29]

Back on Long Island, Evans Griffing, painted a verbal picture of:

> . . . a sailboat going up the bay. Twenty-five feet behind it is a little white dinghy. The five western Towns are on the deck of that sailboat. The five eastern Towns are in the dinghy. Did you ever see a dinghy determine where a sailboat is going? The only way to determine where we're going is to establish a County of our own.[30]

The young man on Ibiza would undoubtedly understand the metaphor.

Stephen Gaskin, Jerry Brown, Barry Goldwater, Karl Hess, Tom Hayden and Evans Griffing understand the unbeatable motivation of self-interest. One's own "turf," is much dearer if one has an opportunity to exert control; thus, citizens are far more likely to participate in self-governance. Apathy arises in the face of distant, all-powerful, state control. Such non-involvement presents not only political, but more importantly, moral and social problems. As the Russian political theorist, Peter Kropotkin, explained in *Mutual Aid*: "unbridled, narrow-minded individualism"[31] is the inevitable consequence of a giant state which has absorbed most primary social functions, and thus released individuals from their obligations to each other.

And Peter Hain in *Community Politics* elaborates:

> This is strikingly apparent in the alienating urban sprawls of to-
> day, where neighborly sharing-out and helping-out has gone by
> the board in a retreat to a narrow "privatized" lifestyle succored
> by remote bureaucratic hand-outs. [32]

So we have come into what contemporary social critic,
Christopher Lasch, has dubbed the "culture of narcissism."
Of the American trend, David De Leon observes that:

> ...our traditional critiques of the existing order have been per-
> vaded by suspicion, if not hostility, toward any centralized dis-
> cipline . . .
>
> The purest essence of this heritage, which has been expressed in
> both individual and communal forms, could be named "anti-
> statism," or more provocatively, "anarchism" . . . we have fre-
> quently assumed that there is an order inherent in nature, that
> society is self-sufficient and that government is likely to interrupt
> the vital functions of individuals and voluntary associations. [33]

American liberalism, according to De Leon, is "burdened
with the modern contradiction that it has often used institu-
tional means to guarantee freedom while popular sentiment
has been deeply skeptical about 'bureaucracy.'" He argues
that both the Right and the Left in this country resist institu-
tional authority and praise decentralized decision-making and
mass participation. He concludes that:

> Americans are not convinced that mammoth systems will neces-
> sarily satisfy their personal needs. Is the modern city more com-
> fortable than neighborhood communities? Is a factory pleasanter
> than a work shop? Is corporate capitalism ecologically, humanist-
> ically and financially desirable? These are issues of the most fun-
> damental radicalness, for which the seemingly exhausted imagina-
> tion of the welfare state and the old left has few answers that are
> attractive to the public.

As "Conservatives" and "Radicals" in this country develop
a common ground, the Independent voter is more likely to
join forces (as Republican and Democratic rolls decline annu-
ally, Independents are the fastest growing block of voters in
the country). Generally, issue-oriented Independents are concerned—at the local and national levels—with questions of
public education, ecology, taxation, health care and social

services, and turned out in droves to vote on California's Proposition 13. In growing numbers, they favor community autonomy and individual self-sufficiency.

In one long-taken-for-granted aspect of American life, which has received recent widespread attention, the efficacy and quality of public education has gone under fire. In Florida tests, high school seniors were found to be functionally illiterate. Numerous books and articles have appeared exhorting parents to educate children at home or through cooperative ventures with like-minded parents. John Holt, educator and publisher of *Growing Without Schooling*, wrote to *The New York Times*:

> The fact is that there are many legal ways of taking one's children out of school and teaching them at home, and that most children learn more, faster and better than children in school . . . . [34]

Holt may be considered radical, but Walter Huss is a conservative from Oregon. After only two weeks as State Chairman of the Republican Party, he, too, opposed the educational bureaucracy: "The biggest sacred cow we've got is education. You talk about it or touch it, you're accused of not being an American." [35] Like every other aspect of American life, education has been institutionalized and bureaucratized to the point of inviolability. Yet, it is buttressed by Government which, in most cases, makes participation compulsory. We have come a long way indeed from Jefferson's *right* of free universal education. This privilege has become a binding requirement to subject young people to an all-too-often inadequate educational system—and, as any taxpayer can attest—it is anything but "free."

Radicals, Conservatives and Independents, all resent the encroachment on every aspect of life by the bureaucratic monolith. Its attendant incompetence and lack of quality has proven frustrating and starkly debilitating. Efforts to reverse these trends in American life are best capsulized in the words of that great proponent of civil disobedience, Henry David Thoreau:

> I quietly declare war on the State, after my own fashion, though

I will still make what use and get what advantages of her as I can, as is usual in such cases.[36]

The marked difference between Thoreau and today's anti-statists is that today's "declaration of war" is not so quiet.

VIII. EXPERIMENTAL MEDICINE

Colonel William Herbert is part-Cherokee and a resident of Brownsville, Texas. He owns a 200-acre island set squarely in the middle of the Rio Grande. Successfully, Herbert and his lawyers have argued that, since the island belongs neither to the United States nor to Mexico, it is sovereign territory. Herbert has named it "Cherokee Nation," and offers citizenship to anyone with any Indian ancestry. If a person wishes to "immigrate" but has no Indian blood, he or she can be adopted. As precedent, Herbert cites Sam Houston's adoption by the Cherokees.

Herbert seceded from the U.S. with a familiar litany: the country has become too big and too complex; lawyers complicate legislation so that it can be interpreted only by lawyers; and American life is dominated by huge organizations and special interest groups. Considering the American Medical Association, as one such group, Herbert has countered with the Cherokee Nation's University and Medical School. Twenty-seven Houston doctors, who oppose AMA domination, have agreed to set up the medical school, financed at a projected $400 million. The campus will comprise ten acres of the island. Courses in all kinds of healing methods, from standard American medical practices to Indian and African techniques, are to be offered.

Another project of Herbert's is to encourage businesses to incorporate under the island's laws which are straightforward and uncomplicated. Ships can be registered in Cherokee Nation, as opposed to Panama or Liberia, to circumvent American legislation. Herbert feels that by promoting commerce on the island, he can improve the general standard of living.

Cherokee Nation is fully autonomous with its own constitution, modeled on that of the United States. It has its own flag, stamps and currency—half-ounce silver and gold coins, with an Indian head on one side and a tepee on the other.

In a wider vector, self-sufficiency and independence are the cornerstones of the American Indian Movement. On Jan-

uary 31st, 1975, in Billings, Montana, wide press coverage
was given to a conference called "Indian Tribes as Emerging
Nations." Howell Raines, in *The New York Times* wrote:

> . . . in the ensuing years, more and more Indians have come to
> think of their reservations as tiny sovereign nations within the
> United States. They look around them and see Third World coun-
> tries becoming rich because of the mineral resources they possess,
> while they still live in poverty on reservations. Ironically, those
> 50 million acres of undesirable and mostly barren lands . . . pawned
> off on the Indians in the last century, contain about one-third of
> the American West's strippable coal, and half of the nation's uran-
> ium, not to mention enough oil to bedazzle the eyes of Texas.[37]

After two hundred years of silence, Indians are claiming
aboriginal title to coal fields, salmon rivers and vast tracts of
land in the eastern U.S. For years, industry and Government
have tenaciously tried to control the wealth on Indian lands
—some 4% of this country—and American Indians have grown
weary of seeing the land destroyed or contaminated. Emma
Yazzle, a Navajo of Fruitland, New Mexico, is still a sheep-
herder at 72, and disdains the brown grass on which the ani-
mals graze. The contamination emanates from the giant, coal-
fired, electric generator at the Four Corners Power Plant.
Emma looks with sorrow at what was once an idyllic summer
encampment: "I want it to be as though I was living a long
time ago. It used to be such a beautiful place. We had all kinds
of colored grass."[38]

In 1975, a Federal Court upheld Indian tribal claims to the
northern two-thirds of the State of Maine. Federal agencies
offered the Passamaquoddy and Penobscot Tribes a settlement of $37 million and 100,000 acres of land. By referen-
dum, the Tribes voted to accept their own negotiating committee's version, which reduced the monetary settlement by
$10 million, but increased the acreage to 300,000. Nothing
has overturned the actual ruling "that Indians have aboriginal
title to lands occupied by Whites who never obtained the Con-
gressional approval required by the long-ignored Indian Non-
Intercourse Act of 1799." [39] Since the Indians cannot undo
the contamination and exploitation of their lands to date,
they, at the very least, demand control over the land's resources. As they gain more control, they also accrue the where-

withal for self-determination.

The Passamaquoddies and Penobscots work arduously at developing their lands, without undermining their culture. Most tribe members speak the Passamaquoddy language, and their schools have a sophisticated bi-lingual program. The Tribes' profits from their timber business are poured into their general welfare, and already a higher standard of living is evident. As Andrew Akins, Penobscot Tribal Administrator explains:

> Whatever is received back, land or money, is not being split. It is in our interest in seeing that a system is set up with the money and the resources generated from the land so that our children will not have to put up with the treatment that our ancestors and we here today have had to.[40]

Across the country, Navajo Nation Chairman, Peter Mac-Donald, of Window Rock, Arizona, has founded the Council of Energy Resources Tribes, or CERT. MacDonald describes it as a "native American OPEC." He views the CERT Tribes as "dependent yet sovereign" nations within the United States. [41] Of this country's resources, CERT owns 50% of the uranium, 15% of the coal, 30% of the low-sulfur strippable coal, 4% of the oil and gas, and substantial portions of the oil shale and geothermal reserves; yet, MacDonald had to approach OPEC to request expert assistance in developing the reservation's resources before the United States Government saw fit to "fill the gap" with $200,000 cash and $2 million in grants.

More recently, *Smoke Signals*, a publication of RAIN (Rights for American Indians Now) announced that the Tribes of the Mohawk Nation, who had settled "Ganienkeh," have won the right to remain there. Originally, the settlement lay on a tract of land in the central Adirondack Mountains of New York State. By dismissing an eviction action in 1977 (after three years of litigation), the state finally restored 5,700 acres of forest land to the Mohawks. A further claim to nine million acres has yet to be resolved.

Smoke Signals[42] reported that:

> ...United States, as well as New York State law, recognizes Indian nations as sovereign entities, at least to the extent that they are immune to suit without consent.

The update in *Smoke Signals* goes on to tell of the new settlement's drive toward self-sufficiency as a sovereign nation. Ganienkeh maintains its own roads with its own, communally-held equipment, has a reconditioned sawmill to aid in home construction, and raises a small dairy herd. Ultimately, the Ganienkehaga plan to run their own fully-equipped school.

Even though "starting from scratch," the residents of Ganienkeh obviously feel that their lives are better preserving not only their culture, but their hereditary rights of governance as well. With control over their own territory, the Mohawk people can at last begin to recover their self-esteem and independence, which have been obscured by centuries of governmental subjugation.

In Vermont, the Abenaki Indians were ordered to appear in court for fishing without licenses. In rebuttal, the Tribal council summoned the wardens who had issued the court citations to answer charges of trespassing on Indian land. This incident clearly dramatizes the incredible difficulty of resolving Indian claims. Yet, continued recognition of the dilemma and persistent dedication to negotiation and resolution must prevail. These once-proud peoples have been subject to the most extreme forms of Government interference and oppression. Thus, it is in the interest of every American citizen that the autonomy and independence of the American Indian be one of the top priorities in a national drive for re-establishment of citizen rights.

Yet another territorial independence move is evident in Puerto Rico. Unfortunately, press coverage concentrates on the terrorist elements in the movement. Interestingly, much of the impetus derives from Puerto Ricans who have lived, or are living, in the United States. Observing first-hand the results of ethnic prejudice and Government inequity, they have surmised that they could vastly improve their lot by controlling their own bailiwick. If one observes the poverty—with all of its related problems—in Puerto Rican ghettos *in this country*, and compares it with the dignity inherent in island village life, the nationalists' case rests most convincingly indeed.

However, the number and amount of American investments

on the island have become the primary impediments to the Puerto Rican Nationalist cause. Fear that businesses and resorts would be nationalized—simple capitalistic self-protection—motivates corporate America's continuing opposition to Puerto Rican independence. Since our country's government is, in largest measure, answerable to the same powers who have holdings on the island, Washington also opposes the Nationalists.

Even for seemingly "mainstream" unoppressed Americans, secession from the country is becoming a theoretical possibility. According to *Yankee Magazine*, John N. Cole, the editor of the *Maine Times* sees a threat in the Federal Government's opening the 300-mile coastline of Maine to disaster-prone tankers and super-tankers. He discerns "patterns which make it sensible to contemplate Maine's rebirth as an independent nation with a new sort of relationship to the Federal government."[43] Undoubtedly, Coles' thinking has been influenced to some extent by the ideas and writings of separatists in nearby Quebec. Nevertheless, not since the Civil War have such provocative pronouncements been made. Yet, Washington apparently regards them as dissentient prattle, and continues to take no notice.

In the United States, concrete action toward secession has manifested itself, so far, only within state and municipal jurisdictions. *The New York Times* of May 13, 1979 reported:

> A secessionist movement is afoot in Westchester County. The "war" is civil, so far, but state and Federal officials fear that it could have widespread fiscal and political repercussions.

> The secessionists are prominent and relatively affluent villages that want to sever their ties from the towns to which they're joined. They want to reconstitute themselves as independent town-villages, gaining a double advantage: cutting taxes for town services that they never receive and, for the time being, putting themselves in line for more federal and state aid.

> Recent village elections in Pleasantville and North Tarrytown . . . overwhelmingly approved separate but identical referendum questions directing village officials to begin the legal process of secession.[44]

When one of the nation's most notable "bedroom" community areas begins investigating, and acting upon, drives for separation, Washington should very definitely sit up and take notice. The residents of Westchester County, New York, have certainly been privy to the "good things" afforded by upper and upper-middle class life in America. These aren't Indians subjugated on barren reservations, nor Blacks locked in opportunity-less ghettos. Yet, even the residents of the green, manicured neighborhoods of Westchester perceive that the only viable direction for future control, and for the cutting back of Government monoliths, lies in gaining some measure of autonomy and independence for their communities.

In Massachusetts, too, secession is being promoted on the state level. According to Henry Beetle Hough, editor of the *Vineyard Gazette*, the movement is in earnest on the islands of Martha's Vineyard and Nantucket:

> Little Cuttyhunk, outpost of the Elizabeth Islands, cast only two votes out of 65 against secession at its annual meeting. Chilmark gave 132 votes for secession to 12 against.[45]

Nantucket, Edgartown and Oak Bluffs followed suit to vote heavily in favor of secession. The two islands had the right of representation 80 years before the convening of the Continental Congress. Thus, when the State of Massachusetts voted to abolish the two representatives to the State House, island separatists began a huge campaign. Secessionist bumper stickers abounded: "Secede;" "Secede Now;" "Free Martha's Vineyard;" "In Our Need We must Sea-Cede Nantucket Island."

Historically, Martha's Vineyard had its own Ambassador to London during the Revolutionary War. And, as Nathaniel Hawthorne observed, during an 1834 visit to the Vineyard, any section of a territory which is indefensible in war must always be allowed "a degree of independence."

While the islanders conduct their campaign with good humor, they have legitimate political and economic grievances. Part of Dukes County has been the lowest income county in Massachusetts for many decades. Hough continues:

> As the director of our Mental Health Center states succinctly, "The islander earns less, pays higher living costs and gets less help

than the citizens of 13 other Massachusetts counties." All rural places suffer in this strongly and selfishly urbanized state, but the islands suffer most and their insularity points up their special plight.[46]

Mandated salary increases for state employees, for which island residents must escrow $125,000, exemplify the islander's plight. A District Court Clerk's salary went from $8,741 in 1972, to $21,117 in 1977. A District Court Judge, from $11,000, to $30,168—paid to a person assigned there only "nominally full-time." Moreover, Massachusetts taxes are very steep; so steep, that, according to *The New York Times*, the state tax level hinders the recruitment of qualified engineering personnel to Massachusetts industry. Appreciating that Vermont taxes are substantially lower, the two islands aim to break ties with Massachusetts and to annex themselves to Vermont.

But even in Vermont, one unhappy county is considering secession from the state. Petitions are being circulated in the five towns on Grand Island, Lake Champlain, where residents are irate at what they deem to be abandonment by the state government. Situated midway between mainland Vermont and New York State, Grand Island is bounded on the north by Canada. It's the only Vermont county with no elected State Senator; and to add insult to injury, its State Representatives were cut from two to one. But, a state decision to abolish the post of Grand Island State Attorney is what, ultimately, engendered the secessionist movement. The voters responded by electing a candidate who promised to maintain an office in the county. The position, as a result, was reinstated.

The New York Times reports that the threat of secession has afforded Grand Island residents some weight in their demands to the state; that "publicity had aroused support and given a sense of legitimacy to the idea." John Curran, author of a separatist petition warns: "The state is going to have to realize that we have been treated badly or we will just keep jabbing them." Curran's petition asserts that secession from Vermont "will help us acquire a strong autonomy and needed economic assistance—maybe foreign aid." Meanwhile, he acknowledges that the movement has a dual purpose, depending on its success: "If we can correct some of these inequities it will make secession less viable. But if we don't, it's an option to be explored." [47]

Other explorations are going on in Edwardsburg, Michigan where a movement called Citizens for Secession was organized to get Cass County to secede from Michigan and to join Indiana, where the business climate is considered better. Support has been mounting and new members, wanting to go further than the founders, are—like their Long Island countrymen—calling for the creation of a new 51st State, to be called Superior. The name itself reflects the growing appreciation that to be autonomous is to achieve a level of existence *superior* to the one permitted by centralized authority.

Keeping things the way they are—or going back to the way they once were—isn't confined to questions of territorial rights, ethnic communities or small towns. Within many urban centers as well, the need for autonomy and self-determination grows evident. Metropolitan centers did not just spring into existence. They derived from the amalgamations of once smaller entities, villages and towns where residents had much greater control over their own lives. Today these neighborhoods wallow in the same slough of two-party power politics and indifferent Government bureaucracy as does every other segment of society. Governmental neglect of urban taxpayers and practices like bank "red-lining" have caused many neighborhoods in major American cities to decay seemingly beyond remedy.

In the City of New York, for example, what is now a prototypical slum, Williamsburg, was once a thriving, affluent community with its own school system. One of the five incorporated towns of Brooklyn, Flatbush, boasted handsome residential streets and the renowned Erasmus Hall High School. Brooklyn, itself, was a dynamic and growing city until it was annexed into the City of New York. Under Manhattan's domination, the borough has seen little but decline. In *Good as Gold*, Joseph Heller counterposes the boarded shops and abandoned tenements of today's Coney Island with the famous-now-gone hotels and restaurants of a glorious Luna Park: the "all year round World's Fair," of an era when stylish people strolled the wide boardwalks.

With neighborhood decay rampant and the actual demise of many cities imminent, urban residents have begun to realize the importance of neighborhood power, as a way of providing accessible, efficient, and effective government. In New York City alone, 59 community boards, whose members are appointed and unpaid, are at work. Fifty members comprise each board, who, in turn, hire city managers to expedite neighborhood dealings with the Greater City—to cut through red tape. According to a 1979 *New York Times* report: " . . . in a little-noticed rearrangement of political and governmental power, these boards are taking on new strengths."*

The boards have lately become arbiters in neighborhood conflicts over the allocation of New York City's now-limited resources. They influence how the City Budget ought to be meted out, and how such basic services as police, trash pickups and parks maintenance ought to be measured and assigned. The boards have even garnered a say in land use. As a spokesman for the City Planning Commission put it: "In 98 percent of the cases before us, we go along with the decision of the community board."

East Flatbush, a neighborhood of neat homes and thriving stores, voted overwhelmingly to oppose the City's designating them as a community qualified for special poverty funds. This astounded Margaret Bald of the Community Development Agency: "This is the first time a community has opposed the designation." Rochelle Tanner, the East Flatbush board's district manager, described the meeting:

> It was wall-to-wall people. They were standing in the hall and standing on tables, and there was not one person who spoke in favor of the designation. We have a community that takes pride in itself. This is not to say the poor shouldn't be taken care of, but not this way. We can relate to individual needs without stigmatizing the whole community.[48]

The population of East Flatbush is both Black and White— about evenly divided. The neighborhood consists of hardworking people, who live in harmony, and who, through block associations and merchants' groups, sustain community pride. The rejection of financial assistance from the City was another step toward neighborhood autonomy; sounding a clarion call for separateness and a willingness to determine local problems, and to solve them on a local, independent level.

In several neglected areas, New York City itself owns many run-down buildings. Instead of serving as the "landlord of last resort," the City has yielded to demands that these buildings be sold to the residents to run as cooperatives. In the South Bronx, where some of these co-ops are located, the people have begun community gardening projects on vacant lots. These developments, in short, enable local residents to feel they have a real stake in the preservation and the betterment of their neighborhood. This, finally, can only enhance both the community and the greater city.

Milton Kotler has articulated well the problems of city bureaucracy as it now exists in most American urban centers: [49]

> Our cities did not grow nicely. Behind the masking rhetoric of a more efficient public service, they grew like political empires by the aggressiveness of central cities annexing surrounding municipalities, wiping out their competition, appropriating their tax revenues, and controlling their territories by police and politics. As these empires grew, downtown prospered in power and finance, while the neighborhoods declined in economic value and public service and welfare.

> During this expansion a new fact occurred. Not to be outdone, state government began restricting and then, taking away power after power from city government; in education, in health, in taxing and bonding, in welfare, and, in some states, in police power. . . . And the neighborhoods, which had always been able to pay for their own administration of public services and welfare, were forced to support the increasingly empty shell of city government and more distant centralized governments, getting decreasing visible benefits for every dollar of tax. . . .

> Neighborhood councils and neighborhood corporations are springing up in all our cities. In the decade ahead, we will see a new struggle for neighborhood rights and local democracy against the abandonment of the people by existing governments. From place to place, neighborhood organization is seeking local control of

schools, welfare, health care, housing code enforcement, police control, revenues and on all fronts of public service.

All of this is proceeding with the full understanding that existing government levels, however inefficient, are not going to simply roll over and transfer authority and revenues to the neighborhoods. But as it becomes more clear that only the neighborhoods can reverse urban decay, the neighborhood movement emerges as a tough process of practical organization, political education, and tactics.

There is more to the horror of this failure than physical decay. The movement of neighborhood control is also a struggle for the liberties and powers to preserve the natural human associations which remain in today's society, and the new forms of associations people are naturally finding together in religion, in friendships, in community, in crafts and humane work. For the neighborhood is still the largest unit in defense of natural association. Should the neighborhoods fail to discover and protect *humane* society, then the best we have to look forward to, by will of powerful government, great corporation, national political parties, and the will of private wealth, is alienation and solitary confinement for all the people.

IX. THE FEVER BREAKS

Neighborhoods rise for self-preservation against cities, cities against counties, counties against states. Yet, above all, the Federal Government directly and primarily affects every citizen of the United States, often leaving him feeling powerless, yet angry, and provoking the spectre of an uncaring, self-serving "they," against whom "we" must struggle.

Some opposition to the Governmental giant is sincere and serious; some seems mere exercise in opposition. But each bears worthwhile lessons. In Wyoming, for instance, in an overt act of defiance, the state overruled the 55-mile per hour speed limit and raised it to 65. State officials have notified Washington that if the Federal Government tries to enforce its own speed limit, Wyoming will withhold the tax on gasoline. Despite overtones of a modern-day Boston Tea Party, this represents a definite reaction to centralized, distant decision-making.

In a more serious vein, the Conservation Committee of the Town of Wendell, Massachusetts sent the President a handwritten letter, penned in splendid Colonial script:

> My Dear Mr. President:
> On May 10th, 1975, the Annual Meeting of the Town of Wendell voted unanimously to prohibit the transport of radio-active fuels, wastes, & nuclear weaponry within the limits of the Town. . . .
>
> . . . It is now reported (see encl.) that the Navy is shiping such waste over the Boston & Maine rails to Idaho fr. the Portsmouth (N.H.) Naval Yards, via Wendell. A *prima facie* case exists for non-compliance, since a similar ban is in force in New York City.
>
> We have therefore written the Navy, the N.R.C., and the Dept. of Transportation, requesting of them their plans for future compliance. . . .[50]

The town of Wendell triumphed. The *Morning Union* of Springfield reported that future transport of used rods from atomic submarines at the Portsmouth Naval Shipyard would bypass Wendell, as a result of the town's opposition.

Four years later, following the accident at Three Mile Island, South Carolina blocked shipment of radioactive wastes into the state from the Pennsylvania plant to the Federal Nuclear Waste Repository at Barnwell. Idaho and Washington are the only other states with Federal nuclear waste facilities, so, were they to take a similar stance, the ramifications would be most provocative to say the least.

Concurrently, the following editorial appeared in Long Island's *East Hampton Star:*[51]

> ... It now seems within reason to hope that the public and local government, shocked into concerted action, will succeed in stopping not only the [nuclear] plants the Long Island Lighting Company wants to build at Jamesport, but also the one it has almost finished at Shoreham. ...
>
> The Lighting Company would reply that we must be kidding, or amazingly naive, to propose leaving unfinished, unused, such a significant project—wasting all that potential electricity and all that money.
>
> And yet, aside from the principle that money thus spent is best left wasted, it has been done before. ...
>
> Which brings us to an idea that is sure to be replete with legal pitfalls, but is worthy of trying. Suffolk County now has a law known as "initiative and referendum" ...
>
> Can the Charter be amended in such a way as to ban nuclear plants in Suffolk? ... Getting enough signatures—about 17,000 would be needed—would not be a problem, we think. Nor would getting enough votes. ... The big hurdle would be litigation, both before and after a successful referendum. ...

In Montana, every proposal for a nuclear power plant must be submitted to the voters for approval in a public referendum. Adopted by a margin of 2 to 1, this statute includes stringent safeguards. In each case, a bond must be posted equal to not less than 30% of construction costs. A working demonstration of a viable emergency cooling system is requisite, as is a proven plan for safe waste disposal. Lastly, license approval must come from a majority of the voters.

With so little known about the long-term effects of low level radiation, let alone the potential for a nuclear catastrophe, it is small wonder that residents in proposed site areas want some say in the matter. One alternative to nuclear plant legislation is local take-over of power companies. On a small scale, this has proved most successful. In Sherill, New York, the new Municipal Power System for 1,300 residents has reduced rates by about 50%. With its initiation in June, 1977, the new system cut rates immediately by 35%, and since then, despite additional cuts, has accumulated a cash surplus of $100,000.

Interestingly enough, the pervasively negative attitude toward power companies is very much part of the secessionist stance. In the 1960's, Rene Levesque pressed for take-over of Quebec's utilities. The creation of Hydro-Quebec saw his objective successfully accomplished. Levesque's keynote slogan during the struggle: "Master of your own house." It is becoming uncomfortably clear that as individuals and communities strive for independence and autonomy, their energy requirements, and disbursements, can no longer be left in the hands of ineptly regulated, profit-hungry, private utilities.

Land use—reclamation, preservation, salvation—has been the impetus for a lot of local action. West Virginia communities, destroyed in floods caused by the rapacious policies of coal companies, decry Federal and state inaction. In Mingo County, the 7,000 inhabitants of Williamson will no longer sue for damages in costly, drawn-out court cases. They are tired of facing hordes of lawyers thrown up by big business. Instead, they have established their own agency, empowered to condemn the land coal companies won't sell. Disaster wrought by corporate greed, and exacerbated by Government inaction, has forced these people to stand on their own—to act in self-defense and self-interest.

Across the country, unfolds a more common, but equally deleterious scenario—the gobbling up of agricultural land by developers. Pastoral settings become apartment complexes, or industrial parks, or shopping malls. As the world's energy and resources decline, so does its wherewithal for food production. Since a society bases its independence on the ability to produce its own provender, it becomes imperative that more careful thought be given to the allotment of agricultural acreage; that more space be preserved in the face of unwanted, often unneeded, development. People must rise to defend the future against the impulse of today's profit incentive. As politicians debate under the sway of various conflicts of interest, more and more land simply disappears. Once again, I & R, or the town-meeting form of government, would allow many instances of possible land abuse to be made public and to be decided upon by those most affected. Undoubtedly, involvement of the general citizenry would hasten promotion and utilization of sound policies.

In the light of unwanted development, and to preserve open space, some communities have adopted ordinances restricting further growth. Ramapo, New York has instituted a plan to slow the pace of any changes, so as to preserve community identity. Often attacked as restrictive or discriminatory, such plans proliferate, nevertheless, as development continues and resident pressure mounts. Oregon has originated a state-wide plan for saving farmland. Whatever the local impetus or motive, most people feel they have the *right* to preserve the essential nature of the place in which they live. By dwelling there, they should have some hegemony over their locale—and this sensibility overrides corporate profits, or Governmental interference.

For minority peoples, particularly Blacks, this feeling of essential power, derived from the land, has usually been decimated. Over and above the various "Back to Africa" movements and Stokley Carmichael's proposal that Louisiana, Mississippi and Alabama be established as a separate Black nation (which have been characterized by some as "extremist"), territorial sovereignty, civil rights, independence and equality of opportunity have been the aims of a widespread, hard-fought struggle. In recent years, these have led to such developments as the Black Panthers' work for community autonomy—particularly in urban areas where Black communities often exist as cities-within-cities. If these predominatly Black sections can gain some measure of control, at least at the local level, then real thoroughgoing self-determination will follow. The statistics of the Emergency Land Fund of Atlanta show that, in 1910, Blacks owned more than 15 million acres of land in eleven southern states. By 1975, despite increases in the Black population, that acreage had shrunk to fewer than 5 million acres throughout the same states.

Currently, in Georgia, an exiled Black community is fighting to retrieve its land in a situation that is most illustrative of our times. Contending that the U.S. Army stole it from them, about thirty people—most of them elderly—peacefully invaded a Federal wildlife refuge at Harris Neck. During World War II, the Army did appropriate the land for an emergency air base. Before the War, Harris Neck had been a community of coastal Blacks who "farmed small plots, raised a few pigs, chickens and cows, and fished in the surrounding tidal waters for shrimp, oysters and blue crabs." Edgar Timmons, Jr., a spokesman for the group, told *The New York Times*: "My parents never had to buy anything from the store but flour."[52] The Harris Neck "invaders" say that they will remain on the land until the Government gives it back, pays $50 million in damages, and rebuilds the homes, churches, schools and small businesses razed by the military.

James Campbell, 76, recalls that before the military incursion, his family lived on ten acres, within sight of the river bank. His father had operated an oyster cannery. One Sunday, Government men told the Campbells to leave, or their house would be pushed down and burned immediately. The Campbells were paid $490 and told they could come back to reclaim the land after the War. With a rented mule and wagon, Campbell moved his family and possessions as military personnel bulldozed his home and fields. Like many of their displaced neighbors, until they found a home, the Campbells had to sleep on the ground and cook over open fires.

For fifteen years after the War, the county controlled the land. In the 60's, the General Services Administration reclaimed it. Subsequently, the Department of the Interior took it over, then ceded it to the Wildlife Service. Now, the Wildlife Service insists it will keep it.

Georgia Representative Bo Ginn has tried to get legislation adopted which would enable the dispossessed residents to buy back their land at the same rate paid by the military—$10 an acre. Since the bill died in committee, Congressman Ginn fears another Wounded Knee.

Exasperated, angry, the people of Harris Neck have finally taken matters into their own hands by reclaiming what was theirs. The act of occupation has landed several of them in jail. Although military confiscation of land, or removal of residents (as was the case in California during the War, when Japanese-Americans were incarcerated, and their fertile lands impounded) occurs rarely in American history, it nevertheless eloquently demonstrates the real power of a centralized Government, as the American Indians would certainly attest. Still, numerous instances of disruptions in many communities by Government, big business, or private wealth have taken a toll on the American psyche. People now realize that they must exert primary control over their land, since government functionaries and corporate interests can but subvert what the citizenry reveres. This assertion embodies a strong movement for local control.

Whether as a result of a local anti-nuclear stance, or anger over misuse of land, or high taxation, or inept representation, most American feel alienated from their Government. This malaise crosses most societal lines—ethnic, geographic, economic. It infiltrates metropolitan areas, farming communities and suburbs; Indians, Blacks, Hispanics, and all those who feel manipulated and repressed. The people of this country are growing weary of vague notions of "Americanism" and a bland "Wonder Bread" culture, wherein each person sees the first slice of his paycheck go to the Federal Government. This state of affairs has produced a pronounced hostility toward central government, which extracts from its citizens, without serving their needs and desires. Current grass-roots movements— for secession, independence or local autonomy—all reflect growing awareness of the inescapable desire for individual responsibility and self-actualization.

NOTES TO PART TWO

1. "Think Small" New York Times, December 21, 1978.
2. (New York Times, December 21, 1978) Ibid.
3. New York Times, December 23, 1978.
4. New York Times, February 23, 1979.
5. New York Times, September 12, 1977.
6. New York Times, 1979.
7. New York Times, 1979
8. New York Times, March 1, 1979.
9. New York Times, July 24, 1978.
10. New York Times, February 3, 1979.
11. New York Times, January 26, 1979.
12. New York Times, May 20, 1979.
13. New York Times, 1979.
14. New York Times, December 21, 1978.
15. Translated by Henry Reeve, revised by Francis Bowen, and edited by Phillip Bradley (Alfred A. Knopf, Inc., New York 1956, Copyright Alfred A Knopf, Inc., 1945).
16. Rattray, The South Fork, Random House, N.Y., 1979.
17. Southampton Press, May 17, 1979, p. 5.
18. Norhoff, The Communist Societies of the U.S., John Murray. London 1875, Schocken Books, New York, 1965.
19. "The Meaning of Being Radically American," New York Times, January 26, 1979.
20. New York Times, April 13, 1979.
21. Copyright 1977, by The Book Publishing Company, 156 Drakes Lane, Summertown, TN 38483, Excerpted from *Volume One: Sunday Morning Services on the Farm* by Stephen Gaskin, p. 49.
22. New York Times Magazine, 1974.
23. Ibid.
24. Gaskin, Vol. I, Sunday Morning Services on the Farm, The Book Publishing Company, Summertown, Tenn. 1977.
25. New York Times, January 31, 1972.
26. See Community Politics, Hain, ed., John Calder, Publishers, London, 1976, p. 62.
27. East Hampton Star, February 22, 1979.
28. East Hampton Star, February 8, 1979.
29. New York Times, March 24, 1979.
30. East Hampton Star, April 26, 1979.
31. See Community Politics, op. cit. supra.
32. Community Politics, op. cit. supra, p. 28.
33. New York Times, January 26, 1979.
34. New York Times, January 24, 1979.
35. New York Times, February 19, 1979 A13.
36. Quoted by DeLeon, New York Times, January 26, 1979.
37. New York Times Magazine, February 11, 1979.
38. New York Times Magazine, February 11, 1979.
39. New York Times, April 22, 1979.
40. New York Times, April 22, 1979.
41. New York Times Magazine, February 11, 1979.
42. Vol. 4, No. 4, April, 1979.
43. Yankee Magazine, July, 1977.
44. Smothers, "Breakaway Villages Worry Albany," New York Times, May 13, 1979.
45. Hough, *A Bumper Sticker Affair, Mostly,* Yankee Magazine, July, 1977. Re-printed with permission of Yankee, Inc.
46. Ibid.
47. New York Times, January 14, 1979.
48. New York Times, March 23, 1979.
49. Kotler, "How Brooklyn Grew," New York Times, February 1, 1972.
50. Reprinted in Clamshell Alliance News, Vol. 3, No. 4, February/March, 1979.
51. April 5, 1979.
52. New York Times, May 1, 1979.

PART THREE

THE PROGNOSIS

X. PRESCRIPTIONS

Karl Hess delineates a radically new system:

> As for general governance, to the extent it is needed and only to that extent, the neighborhoods are ideally suited for government by assembly, for participatory democracy, for town-meeting government. The role of larger, regional or even continental government in a land of free, fraternal communities would be simply that of cooperation or, while national interests persist in the world at large, the role would be one of representing the communities as a Federal emissary or, woefully, as a Federal coordinator of defense forces composed, on the Swiss or Chinese models, of local citizen soldiers based and rooted in the neighborhoods themselves.[1]

Secessionists argue for less and less government, and for virtually total decentralization. And to some, the word secession conjures images of violence—of bomb-throwing anarchy. The primary question, then, is whether or not separatist movements are viable within the framework of the existing American system. Two observations pertain in response. First, "anarchist" in no way describes the kind of people who are now striving for independence and autonomy. Second, few real legal obstacles hinder most secessionist objectives.

Breaking away from larger units means following the provisions of state constitutions where applicable and disregarding those portions which run counter to the Federal Constitution. Increased home rule in communities and neighborhoods will require a change in many municipal laws and the further amendment of most local charters. Originally, towns and villages created and vested the states as legal entities. Now, however, the tables are turned, and the smaller units are construed as creatures of the state, from which their powers devolve. Changes in state constituions could be made to return power to the local level. This would necessarily reduce the authority of the state government. Hence, these forays would have to emanate from the localities, as legislators are notoriously loath about curtailing their own powers.

Article IV, Section 3, Paragraph 2 of the United States Constitution gives Congress the discretion to grant independence to American territories. But as to the relationship between the Federal Government and the states, however, the Constitution is silent. Thus, in 1860, the southern states asserted that federation was a voluntary matter and that each state had the inherent right to secede. The Tenth Amendment reinforces this position:

> The powers not delegated to the United States by the Constitution, nor prohibited by it to the States, are reserved to the States respectively, or to the people.

Thus, conceivably a Constitutional Convention or Amendment could be utilized to permit secession, as neither faces any legal bars. Sentiment along these lines is growing.

Edward J. Woodhouse, of SMU, believes that "simply to undermine Americans' unreflective allegiance to the Constitution of 1787 would be an enormous contribution to future political creativity."[2] To counter the argument that this would result in loss of liberty, Woodhouse avers:

> The nearly uniform opposition to such a convention by liberal intellectuals appears unwarranted. The prevailing fear is that a convention might reduce hard-won civil liberties, including rights to abortion, but it is unlikely that amendments introducing severe deprivations of currently accepted civil liberties could achieve ratification by three-fourths of the states.[3]

Constitutional reassessment could bring the Bill of Rights to bear on communities in the kind of co-federation which Karl Hess envisions. Article IV, Section 4, guaranteeing each state a republican form of government, could be changed to ensure, instead, a *democratic* form of government, effecting a town-meeting system instead of representation. In short, radical changes are possible, within the parameters of the existing system. The Second American Revolution would involve the transformation of the nation into smaller, autonomous and responsive units.

Unfortunately, in some circles, direct democracy is a suspicious, even untrustworthy item. Bureaucrats and politicians persist in the belief that "ordinary people" don't have the intelligence to make the decisions which govern their lives. In fact, bureaucrats contend that even elected representatives lack the skills and information necessary for determining policy. So, entrenching themselves, bureaucrats make access to information as difficult as possible for both legislators and the general public.

Our national energy policy—the number-one area in which bureaucrats and politicians have "botched it"—is riddled by the cross-forces of Government inaction and corporate malefaction. To complete the picture, add a dash of obfuscation from all sides. "Alternative" energy sources, such as sun, wind, geothermals, and sea, are met with vehement resistance in established Government circles, precisely because they enhance the practicality of decentralization and direct democratic participation. As elucidated by Brian Martin in the British publication *Undercurrents*:

> It is becoming increasingly accepted that the reasons for the development, choice and promotion of particular forms of technology are as much political and social as they are technological and economic. Particular technologies tend to lead to particular types of social and political change . . . Therefore, technologies are selected in large part because they serve the social, political and economic goals of those who promote them . . . [4]

Even within the private sector, some segments are now beginning to realize that conventional energy sources must be replaced. Oil reserves are fast-depleting and non-renewable. Technological and environmental problems arise with both coal and nuclear material. Meanwhile, the direct conversion of solar energy into electricity is possible with the photovoltaic cell, and solar power is gaining wider and wider use for heating air and water systems. As Ronald Peterson, President of Grumman Energy Systems, explained:

> I believe solar has a bright future. Some energy analysts believe that within a few years we will be a billion dollar industry. If we have a flourishing market, we can make major contributions to the problems of energy supply, balance of payments and unemployment. But we cannot reach any of these goals if the Departments of Energy and Housing and Urban Development continue business as usual. [5]

Still, the Federal Government continues to downplay the efficacy of solar energy as a power source. Perhaps the old saw is true that once one of the utilities owns the sun, solar energy will be viable, accessible—and high-priced.

The citizens of Pacheco Pass, California, have by-passed the Government to construct 20 windmills, which supply power to 1,000 people—a saving of 175,000 barrels of oil a year. Stressing the need to renew development of the old technology of windmills, David Rittenhouse Inglis, Professor Emeritus of Physics at the University of Massachusetts, contends the truth about the real feasibility of windpower has been withheld from the American people, because the Government has stacked its chips on nuclear energy:

> In keeping with this view, the Federal wind power development program has taken seven years (and is still not quite finished) producing commercial electric power from a megawatt-scale windmill. a feat that was accomplished in two years in Vermont by a small York, Pa. firm about 40 years ago.[6]

Another option opens by harnessing sea waves for power. A New Jersey entrepreneur, Charles A. Peterson, Jr., has received a patent for his sea-powered generating device, which consists of a control tower "closed at the top, and a number of conduits with their lower ends in the water. Waves cause a flow to the top of the tower, and the collected water, running down, operates a turbine, and generates electricity."[7] On a miniature scale, any running stream can create energy when conducted through a generator. Currently, this system is utilized in many African villages, where "appropriate technology" is favored over large, expensive set-ups.

America's continued emphasis on large, centralized technology, requiring sophisticated engineering and technical personnel, derives from the protection of vested privilege—both in the professional and the investment segments of socety. Thus, smaller energy systems, which can be controlled and operated locally, strike at two levels, undermining the basis for such privilege and promoting decentralization and independence. Our general economic hardship and the ballooning cost of fossil fuel energy are forcing the expansion of alternative sources. As necessity furthers independence from centralized energy systems, autonomy becomes increasingly feasible.

In the light of a new society, the computer presents a fascinating aspect of the technological revolution. Often feared as a dehumanizing influence, the computer is actually a boon to the cause of direct democracy, closing the distance-time ratio our society has created. While town-meeting governance worked for small New England towns, some question its viability for urban centers or spread out suburbs. In the very near future, however, virtually every household will probably have a computer terminal, operating through a television set, fed orally or by typing on a keyboard.

The British have instituted a network called Viewdata. It provides subscribers with a keyboard attached to a modified television set. By simply phoning the central data bank, the subscriber can have requested information displayed on the TV screen. According to a *New York Times* report:

> ...Viewdata will enable subscribers to call up computer files on topics ranging from travel advice and recipes to education and finance. Then, too, as envisioned, subscribers will be able to buy department store goods, book airline tickets and eventually send messages back and forth ... 8

Ultimately, then, homes with such systems could communicate with each other as well as with any other place where information is stored. In other words, the town-meeting would not only be possible, but on a much wider scale than in the New England communities.[9] And people will be able to make decisions on a much greater range of issues, based on much better information. As John Garret and Geoff Wright explain in *Undercurrents*:

> The system would be ideally suited for democratic decision-making ...What the domestication of computers means is that the computer is rapidly becoming available and comprehensible to the ordinary person ... A decentralized society needs a very fast and efficient decision-making system, involving all those who might be affected. The traditional democratic method of delegate conferences, as many have experienced, can end up to be slower and more hidebound by rules than central direction. Communication networks should allow decision-making to be faster, more responsive to events, and theoretically enable all members of a unit to be consulted rather than just one delegate. Politics could become the day-to-day occupation of the many rather than the personal gamesmanship of the few.[10]

So powerful is the home computer trend that IBM has begun producing small computers, rather than concentrating on solely large ones. Instead of a few centers collecting stored information, there will be many, with smaller machines, intercommunicating electronically.

At Harvard, the new curriculum makes knowledge of computers mandatory for obtaining a degree. Conversance with computer science will soon be a basic part of literacy. Yet, because the new generation of machines is so simple to use, the mystique will have been dispelled.

Just as the printing press made possible the proliferation of books and literacy, the general use of computers will give greater numbers of people more diverse information than they have ever had before. Moreover, they will be able to communicate with each other more completely and more rapidly. The home computer may very well be the primary instrument in the abandonment of our current representative system and in the installation of direct participation. As E.F. Schumacher posited in *Good Work*, "the bigger the better" is no longer a sound maxim for technology. A truly sophisticated and viable technology can make advancements small enough that everyone has access to them.

If effective decentralization is realized, there remains the provocative question of the threat of foreign domination. The military, by nature, is centralized and designed along heavily bureaucratic lines. How, then, would small autonomous communities cope with the threat of force from abroad?

Hess argues that an alliance of small, well-disciplined and highly-motivated armies is the best possible defense for the country. The war in Vietnam showed us that the Draft was obsolete; that many soldiers would not violate their conscience; that drug abuse, "fragging"[11] and desertion were profoundly disunifying forces. That a volunteer military has proved less than overwhelmingly successful relates as strongly to apathy, as does low voter turn-out. Few will risk their lives to save a country for which they will not even go to the polls. Additionally, vast military resources have proved useless in the Iranian crises. Moreover, we maintain our gigantic military complex at a staggering cost. Admiral Rickover has pointed out that this exorbitant price results from the machinations of sophisticated lawyers, who renegotiate defense contracts for their corporate clients, to enrich both the clients and themselves. This multi-billion dollar expenditure would be controlled if each locality voted its own contribution to the common defense.

The end of our vast military programs does not necessarily mean a loss of jobs. One example of successful conversion is the Brookley Air Force Base near Mobile, Alabama. When the base closed as a military operation in 1969, townspeople dreaded an onset of huge unemployment. Now, however, the people in the area wouldn't take the Air Force back if, as *The New York Times* stated: "the Government came begging." [12] Converted into a prosperous industrial-aviation-educational complex, the installation now provides more jobs than the military ever did. In the words of retired Chief of the Army Corps of Engineers, Lt. General Walter K. Wilson, Jr.: "In my opinion, we are a lot better off now." *The Times* concluded:

> Around the nation, many communities that lost military installations have shared Mobile's experience of renewal. Few want to return to dependence on the Department of Defense, with its fluctuating needs for facilities and manpower. [13]

In addition to ruminations on the military consequences of decentralization, a further question occurs as to the fate of federally-funded social programs. In actuality, most communities pay more Federal tax dollars into existing "human welfare" coffers than they ever get back. Realistically, if money were kept within a locality, it is probable that the area's inhabitants would be at least as compassionate as Congress, and probably more astute than civil servant social workers. In brief, community programs would undoubtedly be superior to those now managed by federal and state agencies.

As has often been proposed, many humanistic programs can be operated more on a basis of volunteerism than by paid personnel. Volunteers could come from all segments of society, but the heaviest concentration would most probably be among the retired and the young.

Health and educational affairs could be local concerns,

thus handled more efficiently and responsibly. In the area of education, volunteers again could greatly enrich the curriculum. Each locality would be able to determine its best mix of intellectual and vocational education, so that they would complement each other. Training in life skills, languages, fine arts, could all be taught based on community interest. The possibilities are, indeed, limitless.

While meeting military needs would be a duty for each community, the management of vital life concerns—social welfare, health, education—would be a *right* of self-governance, and, as far as most Americans are concerned, happily so. These are all matters which intimately and directly bear on the quality of life, and, as such, are best determined by and designed for the locality.

In all of this, it is difficult to foresee the exact form communities in the Hess-defined confederation might take. Certain Constitutional standards, like the Bill of Rights, should apply, but here, similarity to today's society might end. Communities might resemble traditional New England towns, or be constructed like The Farm. In any event, one can assume each one would take on characterisitcs which were direct results of its geography and its inhabitants.

Local volunteers could man town or neighborhood fire departments (as they already do in most small American communities) and help to reduce the size of police forces—something which would be facilitated as well by lower crime rates resulting from close-knit societies.

Instead of a complex system of varying forms and levels of taxation, a single local tax might suffice, with the community, in turn, making contributions to coordinating levels of government. Such a tax should be a straightforward, simple assessment, based on ability to pay, without "loopholes," and applicable to both local residents and corporations.

Community self-sufficiency, buttressed by the adoption of a far simpler lifestyle would promote the greatest possible degree of independence. The less dependent people are on any structure or organization for goods and services, the less power that entity has over them. Self-sufficiency would mean enlightened land use, increased local farming, and reduction of consumption through sharing, planning and frugality. This evokes Thoreau at Walden Pond. But more recently, this kind of life is being realized by Scott and Helen Nearing in Vermont and more recently, in Maine. The Nearings, pioneers in the back-to-the-land movement have lived to an advanced age in excellent health, growing all their own food. They attribute this to their own form of secession—a refusal to do the kind of work which has made human beings cogs in a giant industrial machine.

Another example: a father and his teenage daughter, who have renamed themselves Frank and Dolly Freed, after dropping out of conventional society to live off the land in Pennsburg, Pennsylvania. In one year, they spent only $268.89 on food, out of the $1,400 jointly earned. They make their own whiskey and dandelion wine, and have developed a "fiercely strong strain of laziness"[14] which Dolly considers quite healthy. In fact, the Freeds have come to realize that people hardly need work at all once they master the art of self-sufficiency and overcome the excessive need for material possessions. Dolly Freed has written a book called *Possum Living* about their lifestyle. As Frank Freed expresses it: "It's so easy to live without a job, it's pathetic."[15]

Autonomous communities, being small in area, will make cycling and walking more common than driving cars. This, with resultant lower levels of pollution, of course, will contribute to better health. Downtown revitalization and the concentration of population would obviate much of the ugly strip-zoning along highways. Modest forms of public transportation could convey people from one population center to another.

In their present embryonic form, these communities are actively conservational, an approach which will become even more widespread. The physical character and aesthetic of a place lie as much at the heart of this phenomenon as does concern for healthy environment.

Aesthetic regard has already led many American communities toward a kind of cultural self-sufficiency. Common are local associations of poets, writers, artists and musicians; local theatre proliferates. Television and film provide access to great performances by artists of international calibre, precluding the necessity of "big city life."

But something even deeper underlies this overview. As Stephen Gaskin has said:

> There is an ongoing search for the holy. Not only a search, but once you've had a taste of it, you have to have some more of it, and find out how to get closer to it.[16]

Decades of materialism have whetted an appetite for the spiritual. People find they need renewed the sense of community as a foundation for their lives.

The kinds of interaction possible in small communities tend to undermine segregation on the basis of race, age or wealth. Additionally, recognition of the value of everyone's contribution to the community alleviates societal tensions. As its pace is slowed, life becomes more precious, with human association its most valuable aspect.

How, then, does a community lay the bases for political autonomy? One option is, of course, to declare itself non-profit, or religious, as did The Farm. Another is to be adopted by an Indian nation, thereby becoming a virtual sovereign entity, immune from suit and exempt from many Federal laws, including those of the Internal Revenue Code.

In most cases, governmental structure would probably fall along lines of the town-meeting concept, including recourse to I & R, thereby viewing political stewardship in several new ways. Candidates, for instance, should perhaps all run for office as independents, thus rendering political parties obsolete. Officeholders might receive compensation based on their performance in office, and any officeholder violating the public trust would be subject to recall and would go unremunerated. Such practices would preclude the abuses of special interests and the influx of greedy politicians. Bedford, New Hampshire has already demonstrated the feasibility of such an approach. At the Bedford town meeting, the people voted not to pay their Aldermen because one had been voted permission to operate a real estate business in a residentially-zoned area.

Even the City of New York has heard numerous demands for amendment of the City Charter to allow recall of the Mayor and other public officials. Some localities already have the authority to recall judges.

Ideally, direct vote of the people should decide most matters in a community, including fiscal matters such as taxes and budgets. With real control, direct democracy works, and it works best in small communities.

As Karl Hess has said:

> My own position is in favor of participatory democracy. Representation in politics is rather like representation in love. It only works in the theoretical sense. . . . None of this, of course, means that I would deny any other non-aggressive group of dopes the right to go ahead and have their own theocracy, representative democracy, monarchy, or what have you. It should be a matter of choice in a free society, and a free society, in turn, seems to me only possible in discrete units, communities, where a society is possible as opposed to a corporate state. . . .17

The things the secessionists want—life based on spiritual values; full integration of all age groups, with the old given positions of leadership and veneration, and the young, increased responsibility; a kind of continuing "celebration of life"— may sound Utopian. Yet, ideally, each community would be a Utopia; a free and independent nation. This frames the real America, the one to which most people have always aspired.

Once one begins to analyze objections and resolve problems, the possibilities become apparent. Under our present system we suffer one abuse after another. It seems inane to continually ask "WHY?"—exhilarating, for a change, to dare "WHY NOT?" Since the introspection of the 70's and the revelations of Watergate, the burden of justification has shifted to the system itself. To date, it has certainly not made a convincing case. Advances in technology are making decentralization and participatory democracy most attractive. At the same time, a renewal of humanistic values is rendering current forms of government obsolete.

XI. THE CONVALESCENCE

Despite the prospects of increased autonomy and a far better life for Americans, strong resistance will undoubtedly crop up. Professional politicians, party leaders, elected representatives and bureaucrats—from local school administrators to nuclear regulatory personnel—will not gleefully relinquish their positions. *The New York Times* described this phenomenon as it manifested itself on Long Island:

> In Nassau, both Republican and Democratic politicans who professed to favor voter initiative and referendum, delayed and dodged, postured and posed until they had for all practical purposes killed no fewer than four such proposals.

> In Suffolk, the Republican-dominated County Legislature rejected Suffolk County Executive John V.N. Klein's effort . . . to have voter referendums on taxes and spending this year.

> Although most politicians still prefer to remain silent on voter initiative and referendums, or at best give lip service to the principle, officeholders of both parties from Governor Carey on down don't want the voters second-guessing their fiscal decisions or restricting their fiscal maneuverability.[18]

The politicians' justification of their existence often derives from Thomas Hobbes. To wit, a contract exists between them and the people, and that their job is to govern, while the people conduct their own lives. In addition to being Hobbesian fans, politicans revere "order"—both as a word and concept. Henry Kissinger even quoted Goethe to the effect that any order was better than none.

Certain flaws, however, predominate in this thinking. First, according to Hobbes, the social contract exists between a sovereign and his people. But, this doesn't obtain in the United States. On the contrary, this country rests on the principle that the people were sovereign. Moreover, the Founding Fathers, while respecting order, certainly placed liberty as the premium possession—at any price.

Representatives in this country are ostensibly selected according to the tenets of John Locke; i.e., to act *on behalf* of the people who elected them. Bureaucrats, derivatively, exist to execute the instructions of the people, as borne by their representatives. Representatives and bureaucrats hardly qualify as sovereign. Rather they were intended as stewards—custodians of the public trust. Elected officials supposedly govern with the consent of the sovereign people. They do not "rule."

Unfortunately, practice shows that representative democracy usually belies its name. Once placed in power, legislators or appointees assume all of the trappings of sovereignty—even to the extent of divine right. Elections and endless court cases cannot dislodge them. Prejudicial election laws make third party or independent candidacies painfully difficult. Thus, the struggle to renew democracy, now that the realization of the various dilemmas has arisen, will likely encompass civil disobedience at the very least.

The perpetual strain of trying to make governmental or corporate bureaucracy do something—or refrain from doing something—eventually takes its toll in frustration and disillusion. From the anti-nuclear Clamshell Alliance at Seabrook, New Hampshire, to Harris Neck, Georgia, acts of civil disobedience wax more common every day. As these incidents proliferate, the general public is more sympathetic to the "agitators," mirroring its own disgust of government. And, the average citizen begins to perceive civil disobedience as the only recourse against governmental insensitivity and abuse.

Beyond its potential for effectiveness, civil disobedience, under some circumstances, may, ironically, be legal. In Oregon, the defendants in a case of protest at the Trojan nuclear plant were acquitted after presentations were made on the dangers of nuclear power. A memorandum of law in the case stated:

> . . . the evil of the threatened injury far outweighed the evil of the alleged violation of the trespass statute. The practice of peaceful public protest has been sufficiently widespread in the last century to identify it as an important catalyst for American social and political reform. Sensitive and thoughtful Americans have used forms of civil disobedience as part of the effort to end the Mexican-American War, repeal the Fugitive Slave Act, improve working conditions for laborers, achieve voting rights for women, enact a Civil Rights Act of 1964 and withdraw United States troops from Southeast Asia . . . The question is no longer one of pure and abstract morality when the defendants take action based on a belief that direct and immediate harm is emanating from a nuclear plant

> in the community . . . It is ultimately the jury, the representatives of the community, who must decide if the defendants are blameworthy for their conduct . . .

Because most Americans have no first-hand experience in civil protest, the most common form of rebellion is impulsive and personal. A typical example: the Californian in a long gas line, who drove to the front of the line, pulled a gun, filled up his tank and drove off. Now, however, disgusted with traditional party politics, people may well start saying: "Why not take some form of community action?" "What about a tax strike?" As Americans communicate and organize, the Government may very well find that it indeed has something to worry about.

In a growing number of cases, punishment for civil disobedience actually offers a source of pride—a badge of courage. Four people from Harris Neck served jail sentences of 30 days as the result of actions taken before a night meeting to plan "picket lines and other demonstrations, fund-raising efforts and the organizing of the 60 percent of the population that is black to take control of political offices in McIntosh County."[19] According to *The Times*:

> They did not lament the fact that four of their leaders were still in jail for trespassing . . .
>
> "I have a son in jail and I am happy about it," said a 61-year old minister, the Rev. Christopher McIntosh, Sr., "because the good master is answering our prayers."

The people of Harris Neck concluded, after 37 years of waiting, that they would have to fight to reclaim their land. And to succeed, they might have to take over the whole county and run it themselves.

In Montague, Massachusetts, North East Utilities erected a tower to test wind speeds in preparation for the construction of a nuclear power plant. Sam Lovejoy toppled it singlehandedly in an episode that has come to be known as "Lovejoy's War." The plant has been postponed indefinitely.

On Long Island, the SHAD Alliance (Sound and Hudson Against Nuclear Development) openly discussed plans to occupy the Long Island Lighting Company's Shoreham nuclear plant, which is 80% complete. *Suffolk Life* reported:

... SHAD is training about 200 persons, including housewives, mothers, priests, nurses, writers and poets, in "non-violent civil disobedience action." They are being trained in groups of 18 to 20 persons, who will stay together during the occupation and operate under a group leader.[20]

Additionally, signs in the area announce a "legal" demonstration as well, for those who do not feel ready for civil disobedience.

All of these constitute direct actions in defense and support of a community. As more communities go under the gun, more and more actions of this type will occur. When people act together in community defense, they manifest the secessionist spirit, which is as old as the country itself. Before American independence, Vermont broke away from Massachusetts. In 1794, farmers of western Pennsylvania threatened to secede because of the Whiskey Tax. During the War of 1812, which was extremely unpopular in New England (just as the Vietnam War would be a century and a half later), three New England states threatened to make a separate peace with England. During the Civil War, the southern states seceded, and, in that process, West Virginia broke away from Virginia. More recently, and on the local level, Nassau County split from Queens, when the latter opted to join the City of New York. Currently, two active secessionist movements are at work on Long Island.

Implicit in this spirit is a defiant anti-government stance, which dates back to Shays' Rebellion. In 1786 Dan Shays and his followers organized because the Government demanded taxes in specie. A tight money policy existed at the time and the state was unwilling to grant credit or accept payment in produce. Instead, the government seized farmers' land and household goods when they were unable to pay. Angry citizens had convened *ad hoc* conventions and demanded relief, but their petitions went unanswered. In rebuttal, they prevented the courts from sitting, so that tax judgments could not be rendered. Then, the protestors attempted to take over the Federal arsenal at Springfield. Massachusetts could not put down the rebellion and appealed to Congress. Congress, however, didn't have the money for troops. Finally, Shays, and his supporters, were subdued by a privately-financed militia. *200 Years*, a bicentennial history of the United States, analyzed the consequences of the uprising:

> The rebel leaders were pardoned, and most of the reforms they demanded were put into effect. But the rebellion had a chilling effect on the rest of the country. Every state had its disgruntled debtor class, and if such men could take the law into their own hands in Massachusetts, were men of property safe anywhere? [21]

Today, the question may evolve as to whether politicians and corporate moguls are safe anywhere.

With the threat of rebellion hanging over their heads, delegates to the Constitutional Convention in 1787—undeniably "men of property"—subsequently approved a strong, central Government. This despite the fact that the meeting had been convened solely to revise the Articles of Confederation. The debate on the ratification of the new Constitution (which was approved by a close vote of 187 to 168) evinced strong reservations among delegates. The most notable came from Patrick Henry of Virginia.

> Whither is the spirit of America gone? We drew the spirit of liberty from our British ancestors. But, now, Sir, the American spirit, assisted by the ropes and chains of consolidation, is about to convert this country into a powerful and mighty empire. [22]

Jefferson, though not a convention delegate, was extremely skeptical of its outcome. Both James Madison and George Mason opposed it. And, Edmund Randolph asserted that a single executive was "the fetus of monarchy." Despite the dissension of these enlightened men, the Federalists won the day. The United States acquired a central Government, and a Federal bureaucracy. Thus did our Founders protect propertied interests from the "debtor classes."

Then, during Washington's second term, farmers in western Pennsylvania rose in protest against the Government's first excise tax, which was unmistakably aimed at their chief product, whiskey. At first, these independent distillers began terrorizing tax agents and "legitimate" whiskey-makers. Finally, they threatened to secede. Ultimately, the President had to dispatch a force of 15,000 militiamen to quell the Whiskey Rebellion. Some of the routed farmers fled to other states, where they continued to make untaxed whiskey, passing their recipes down from generation to generation. To this day, they daunt the tax collectors. Their product in great demand, they are certainly in no danger of being absorbed by National Distillers. In their own way, they have seceded.

Today, a lot of America belongs to the "debtor class." Even "Middle Americans" view the Federal Government as the pawn of an elite few. And, like Shays, they are in revolt. Similar perceptions pervade the anti-nuclear movement, which avers that the promotion of atomic power serves an elitist, arrogant Government and profit-hungry special interests. Add to the list, angry workers who resent wage guidelines, who advise the President to "Stay the hell away"; small farmers, small businessmen and minorities—all feel the same sense of betrayal. Overt hostility toward the Government even comes from as unlikely a quarter as fishermen. As the *Southampton Press* reported on May 17, 1979:

> Two hundred East End commercial fishermen staged their own version of the Boston Tea Party . . . to protest a new Federal regulation which would require them to keep daily log books recording all their catches of groundfish and herring. Called by the National Marine Fisheries Service to discuss the regulations . . . the fishermen marched into the front of the room barely five minutes after the start of the session and dumped their log books on a table . . . and then marched out en masse.

Warned that the fishermen faced up to $25,000 in fines if they did not comply, Richard Miller, Executive Secretary of the Long Island Fishermen's Association, said:

> Experienced fishermen would have to offer for scrutiny the knowledge and information gathered through years of experience. This information is a trade secret and no businessman should be put in a position of helping competition degrade his business position. Fishermen consider it an affront that government, because of its inability to do the job, mandates by regulation that hardworking taxpayers do it for them. These log books are to be filled out by the harvester, wholesaler and processor. The end result of this added paperwork will mean higher prices for the American consumer and less income for fishermen. The business of the fishing industry is to produce fish for food and not to produce paper for bureaucrats. Government has become more of a deterrent than an assistant in carrying out the goal of feeding people.[23]

From justification of Vietnam to statements on the effects of low level radiation, the Government has lost credibility. Consequently, it is increasingly difficult to characterize detractors as irresponsible dissidents, especially when many of them may be the most highly informed and highly motivated citizens in the country. Farmers and fisherfolk aren't "hippy radicals." They simply want to live and work, free from the strictures of an alien, oppressive Government. They have begun to rally in defense of their own communities as bastions against abuse. In practice, their struggle begins to resemble Shays' more and more and unless substantial reforms are made in time, is bound to move from petition to civil disobedience to violence. Perhaps, the Government should heed the voice of the sovereign people.

The practical application of the secessionist spirit, of course, has its wrinkles to be worked out. For instance, many people tend to abdicate responsibility, while taking their rights for granted. The original New England settlers had a definitive solution to this problem: a fine for non-participation at the town meetings. Democracy was an *absolute*, not a relative value; citizenship alone mandated participation. Without some inherent guarantee of participation, interest is likely to wane, eroding back to the "representative" form of government, then to bureaucracy, and, ultimately, perhaps to a dictatorship. American thinking has become "relative" or pragmatic, a sobering idea. Witness, for example, the abuses incurred in the name of "national security." Thus, the more derivative democracy is, the more relative it becomes. As this occurs, democracy can be set aside more and more easily to meet other "priorities."

Many political thinkers—with Jefferson and Thoreau—acknowledge the right of citizen rebellion; unassailably when human life is endangered for no apparent good reason. Herein falls the war in Vietnam and the current controversy over the development of nuclear energy. At the very least, citizens must have some voice in what constitutes a valid cause for the sacrifices of their lives.

Jefferson perceived that the preservation of liberty meant constant struggle. His attempts at safeguarding freedom encompassed the concept of the mini-republic. Today's secessionists draw upon Jeffersonian ideals, as well as those of Rousseau and Thoreau. For them, the only possibility for a restoration of direct democracy lies in the re-establishment of autonomous communities.

XII. APPLIED THERAPY

The formation of a wholly new society is an awesome task. As "alumni" of the reformist, albeit traditionally-run campaigns of Goldwater, McCarthy and McGovern can attest, the struggle for change seems doomed by insurmountable obstacles. Yet, these obstacles reside in the existing system and must be targeted in any all-out effort to redesign our political system. For instance, most new electees prove as feckless as their predecessors. Despite the large personal investments made by campaign workers and "believers"; despite the fact that the candidate won, the entrenched *status quo* prevails. Now, instead of knocking themselves out in an electoral process, which is almost always disheartening, people are beginning to realize the field of battle lies right in thir own community, and that traditional political practices will, quite probably, avail them nothing.

Such endeavors school one in the futility of directing energy into an already structured set-up. It *will* be diverted, and eventually, lost. Howard Jarvis didn't utilize a bureaucracy to get Proposition 13 passed. He relied on the anger, and the spirit, of the taxpayers. No opposition candidates could dissipate or undermine that kind of energy.

Asked about the fledgling movements to dump him, Lyndon Johnson answered scornfully: "Movement? Most movements consist of a couple of people and a mimeograph machine." If, indeed, this is the case—and in the beginning of most political endeavors, it is—then perhaps, it is the most viable approach to change. The goal remains "paramount"—not organization, not impressive trappings, not personal aggrandizement. The only feasible line of attack on the existing system evolves from the grass roots, not from any existing organization nor any institution.

Of late, the American political system has seemed grindingly quiescent. The reformist spirit of the 60's has virtually disappeared. People and ideas have taken a respite. However, now, particularly since the success of Proposition 13, something bubbles beneath that placid surface. Citizens are angry. They see school programs cut while their property taxes escalate to defray salary increases for administrators. Our national train service has reached an all-time low, just as the energy situation is pronounced critical. Many communities cannot qualify to receive federal funding for necessary programs, because state laws forbid their fulfilling the federal requirements. Despite the growing presence of real rage and hunger for change, past political failures have, unfortunately, made many people wary of once again attempting political reform.

The inspiration for concerted effort often grows from individual actions. Hubert Houston, of Memphis, is spear-heading a nuts-and-bolts revolt against the high cost of repairs to lawn mowers and power tools. His rebellion began when he posted a notice in the Memphis Public Library, offering free technical advice to anyone having trouble with one of those "labor-saving" devices. Houston asserts that too many people pay good money for repairs that are simple enough to be explained over the phone. "If people would just use a little horse sense, they'd keep more money in their pockets," he notes.[24] Although Houston's "campaign" has become well-known in the area, he refuses to charge a fee. Needless to say, he receives countless telephone calls.

As we all know only too well, the cost of everything is going up. At every level, our life structures have become more complex, making independent survival increasingly difficult— if not impossible. Undoubtedly, a few will profit from the coming hard years. Most, however, will suffer. The opportunity for action in concert must be seized to effect freedom from the system.

Such communal action can be most naturally and effectively utilized for essentials. The general public can still control many aspects of food, housing and transportation. As for food, people everywhere will need to rely less on food-producing corporations and more on "communal" efforts. For the many who have no desire to join a commune, or take up farming, the establishment of community food cooperatives, a boon both to price and quality, might be one answer. There is already a Cooperative League of the United States headquartered in Washington, which boasts an ever-increasing membership. My own community on eastern Long Island has formed

United Consumers of the Hamptons. Requisites for the first wholesale buy included an organzation bank account and 250 to 300 members.

People are beginning to exert influence in housing, too. In urban areas, a movement for "tenant power" is spreading. Jeffrey D. Bogart, President of the tenants' association in one New York apartment building, writes: "There are more tenants than landlords who vote. Through a city-wide tenant association, pressure could be brought to bear."[25] Why, then, be a victim of a Rent Board that is held in thrall by city landlords? Tenants can "secede" by saying that their buildings are their communities. Thus, they can insist upon substantial voice in how the buildings are run, and in what rents are both viable and fair. Many cooperatives and condominiums already function this way, governed by resident rules and regulations. There is no reason why renting apartment dwellers cannot devise a similar system.

Believing that Americans were too dependent on government, Jim Davidson, a young Oxford-educated American, founded the National Taxpayers Union. Single-handedly, he first ran his small office on a shoestring and began by raising funds. Going from state to state, he amassed backing for a "balanced budget" Amendment to the Constitution. So far, he has rallied support in thirty states. Now numerous people are working with him around the country. Davidson sees himself as a businessman selling an idea whose time has come; his motto—a quote from John Milton: "There is no better way to spend one's time than in the vindication of liberty."

It is the strength of an idea which generates a movement. The movement, in turn, is promoted with public relations, a knowledge of the law and some understanding of the system. The kinds of endeavor undertaken by Howard Jarvis and Jim Davidson aren't political in the typical sense and, for that reason, they have found support. By and large, people have been put off by traditional politics, and are now seeking alternative methods by which to make themselves heard.

Karl Hess wrote recently:

> I've been working with a gang of friends in Hawaii to get a "none of the above" place on the ballot. I view that as a step toward se-

cession, as a matter of fact. Once people become conscious of how silly most political personality choices are they may become conscious of how very silly most remote politics are in general
. . . .

As for a national movement which, in fact, would encourage communities to act *as though* they had seceded, I see a strong need and response. Perhaps both things go together. I am very shy of exclusive political causes. But I do see the need for rallying points *etc.* Just so the points don't become ideological spearheads . . . .[26]

By creating this "sense of secession," Hess proffers the sort of course he and eighty other people are pursuing in Kearneyville, West Virginia. Their tactics include alternative technology groups (including solar projects), innovative housing, water and wind power, gardening, "even some fanciful ideas for recombinant research to switch some production over to bio- rather than mechano-processes." Such "communal efforts" are reinforced by contact with like-minded people from other communities. This helps to preclude a feeling of isolation. According to Hess, then the Long Island Peconic people should meet with the secessionists from Martha's Vineyard, and so on.

On eastern Long Island, "secessionists" have sponsored an alternative energy fair, square dances and barbeques in order to stimulate support for independence. "Peconic" has moved beyond its conceptual phase to encompass a sense of community, as well as a new politics. In Southampton Town, where most of the leaders of the Peconic County movement come from, several rallies have been held to press for the adoption of the I & R process on the Town level, and I & R advocates are fairly optimistic.

Community identity and an awareness of the bankruptcy of the two-party system is determining the citizen's new approach to politics. Even if the only objective were the introduction of the town-meeting form of government, this in itself would be meaningful and would enhance the instigation of I & R, and finally, secession itself. If enough communities commit themselves to an objective of independence a national anti-Party working to create small autonomous entities would automatically follow. Certainly it is worth trying. Besides, there is no other constructive alternative around at the moment.

XIII. THE ROAD TO RECOVERY

In *The Philanthropic Ogre*, Octavio Paz, the Mexican poet, has written:

> The state has been and is the dominant personality of our century. Its reality is so enormous that it seems unreal; it is everywhere, yet it has no face. We don't know what it is nor whom it is.

Paz sees no distinction between competing types of social systems. "Bureaucratic capitalism" has adopted the vices of "bureaucratic socialism" (and vice versa). "This is the crises of the twentieth century," he explained in an interview. "The state is becoming ever stronger, and we have the paradox that, to defend themselves against Soviet expansionism, to defend democracy, the Western nations are becoming steadily less democratic."[27] Seemingly a balanced critic, Paz recognizes that whether a nation-state is capitalistic or socialistic, the people not running the system are the ones who suffer from the failures and deceits of politicians and captains of industry.

Paz speaks from the vantage point of the left, yet, on the right, such writers and thinkers as Friedrich A. von Hayek, Milton Friedman, Robert Nozick and Maoist-turned-conservative Bernard-Henry Levy, have all denounced the state's interference in the affairs of human beings.

When the social contract of this nation was written, the Federal Government was delegated only a limited authority. Other powers not expressly delegated, remained, according to the Tenth Amendment, with the states or the people. Over the years, that contract has been subtly and deleteriously altered. The people have been left with vastly diminished authority, while the central Government has become all-powerful, all-controlling, pervading every segment and direction in American life. Finally, we are beginning to comprehend the nature of the real dangers inherent in these developments. Americans now realize that they must fight to preserve what little remains of their liberty; to vie with colossal powers to win back some measure of life control.

As both the reality and the sense of community disintegrated in this country, bureaucracy and centralization filled the void. Liberty and quality of life receded in the power shift. In the name of progress, corporations have grown mighty and entrenched. The American citizen no longer runs the business and the Government of his country. Rather, he is ill-used by them in a titanic game with rules he cannot perceive, and aims which concern him not at all.

If Americans are to regain control, they shall have to overcome the handmaidens of Big Business, Big Labor, and Big Government. They must commit themselves to a struggle more herculean than that waged by the original settlers. Today's "pioneer" will not be creating a society in a virgin, flexible context. Instead, he will be attempting to raze powerfully entrenched structures in order to rebuild.

Conditioned as we are to lives of stress and isolation, we cannot easily conceive another existence. Yet, these very qualities so deplored in our everyday existence can be obliterated in true community. Citizens can re-discover the satisfaction of working together for the common good. Senior citizens rescued from inaction and loneliness, nuclear families involved in extended groupings, can taste again the real joy of simple human association.

The kind of political ideal proposed here is only a suggestion, not a blueprint for automatic success. It betokens a possible escape from the endless cycle of frustration inherent in the politics and the lifestyle of Americans today.

Most Americans would avow that they are not political, or that there are no political solutions. This attitude in itself reflects the rampant feelings of apathy and impotence in the country. Citizens see themselves as ciphers. Yet, catastrophes remind them otherwise and evince not only feelings of anger and fear, but desire for control. Daily headlines attest:

ANGRY JACKSON MISSISSIPPI SEEKS SOMEONE TO BLAME IN FLOOD.

UTAH TOWN MORE HURT THAN ANGRY BY SUGGESTION OF DEATH FROM FALLOUT.

FEAR OF SLIDES IN MALIBU HILLSIDE FORCES EVACUATION.

TOWN IS WORRIED BY A LEAKY SILO CONTAINING ATOMIC BOMB WASTE.

The last headline comes from Lewiston, New York, near Niagara Falls, site of the Love Canal debacle. The residents of this area have fallen victim to both private companies and Government agencies. Their nightmare daze is the result of nuclear and chemical contamination; their jobs and homes, threatened or lost; their mortal lives, endangered—let alone those of succeeding generations. If things continue in the current vein, their plight is very possibly a harbinger for the rest of the United States.

Who thinks about the people? Do they "complicate" political theory and practice to such an extent that they are best forgotten? How much abuse must citizens suffer before the system changes in a responsible way or by oppression?

Since outside relief is rare, many people have started doing more for themselves. As they do, they begin to wonder why giant, ineffectual super-structures exist at all. In this complex society, of course, dissenting localities can't assume all Federal functions. Yet, given our diversity of interests with the number of areas and ethnic groups demanding rights and privileges, effective erosion of Federal power seems inevitable. Certainly the people and their Government are on a collision course.

The resultant struggle may produce a period of near-anarchy, but such darkness may be the only alternative to Orwell's 1984. Since the Government is monolithic and costly, without solving significant problems, creating "national policy" will become increasingly difficult. Suspicion and mistrust of Federal management will further retard the adoption of "national" reforms. All this should help force the Federal giant to yield to demands for decentralization along community lines.

The nature of such communities would be determined by many local considerations, particularly by the character and desires of the people who inhabit them. No longer can it be the plaything of special interests and power mongers. It must become the prideful vessel and emblem of a people who live happily with citizen responsibility and freedom. Some creative tension will always run between individuals and their institutions, but it will be acceptable as long as their transactions flow freely back and forth.

The real America is a collection of diverse territories and peoples, and still comprises the best of human aspirations. Of late, though, there is another America, which is little more than a product or a Madison Avenue slogan. The ad campaign to sell it wears thin abroad, while fewer and fewer buy it at home. Faith in a token abstraction isn't enough. In reaction, it seems that faith in the community has begun replacing belief in the whole. If this change of fealty continues, then the component parts will, per force, become stronger and more self-reliant. These parts can be conjoined only as a healthy *new* whole. The new society need never contend with *mass* problems, *mass* consumerism, *mass* hysteria.

Once, in America, local beers—all of them different—abounded. Gradually, a few big breweries acquired all of the smaller enterprises and, one day, every kind of beer tasted like every other. But lately, new beers are being brewed, produced in small quantities, distributed within their own region. Each has its own flavor. And these distinctive beers are selling, forcing the bland giants to launch ever more massive ad campaigns.

These emblematic developments in the beer industry bespeak the doom of our era of gratuitous bigness. One thing can no longer be made acceptable to all. The mentality of reduction to the lowest common denominator—whether in beer, television programming, education or political office-holders —will not suffice.

Now, one begins to witness a metamorphosis in sprawling suburbia with its look-alike tract housing and shopping malls. Houses are being individually remodeled; quaint buildings, preserved and restored. Suburbanites have re-discovered woodburning stoves, home-baked bread and backyard vegetable gardens.

The two-party system addresses itself to "Wonder Bread and Budweiser" America, offering two bland candidates as a "choice." No real issues are confronted, no real ideas proposed, no real questions answered. But as real issues and hard questions draw closer and closer to home, Americans begin to perceive their differences and, more importantly, to realize their options.

The town-meeting form of government and the use of I & R are issue-oriented and spontaneous. They can effect change quickly and efficiently, or rectify and even undo mistakes. Mistakes can be instructional. But under the current system, mistakes are denied; bad judgments, concealed. Government responds by spinning out ever more entangling regulations and bureaucratic forms. The mess compounds, as do the uncorrected mistakes. In such a perpetual snarl, nothing progressive, or creative gets accomplished. Meanwhile, human freedom and human dignity are relegated to the back seat.

Growing awareness strikes the one optimistic note. According to the Committee for Public Justice:

> We have learned that no matter who is President, regardless of which party is in power, our freedom will depend on the efforts of each and every one of us individually.

And from Common Cause:

> It's time for all of us to face the simple truth. . . . The reason the United States Government cannot solve our pressing problems is because the United States Government *is the problem.*

Americans are fed up. They demand control, not a choice between two carbon-copy puppets. Mature freedom accepts responsibility, and must, therefore, include the option for local autonomy and direct democracy. As the nation-state recedes, we stand on the threshold of a new chapter in human history. Although the state seems bigger and more powerful than ever, the old Irish proverb tells us that, "Even midgets cast great shadows when the sun is setting." We can transcend this dusk, and, with the dawn, see a society of participatory, fraternal communities, wherein human will and human dignity prevail.

NOTES TO PART THREE

1. Hess, "Why Neighborhoods Must Secede," New York Times, January 31, 1972.
2. New York Times, April 22, 1979.
3. Ibid.
4. Martin, Soft Energy Hard Politics, Undercurrents No. 27, April-May, 1978.
5. Newsday, March 28, 1979.
6. Letter to New York Times, dated April 5, 1979.
7. New York Times, 1979.
8. New York Times, June 28, 1979.
9. People are already participating in local government meetings in Columbus, Ohio via their two-way television system.
10. Garrett and Wright, "Micro is beautiful," Undercurrents, No. 27, April-May, 1978.
11. Assassination of ranking officers
12. New York Times, April 26, 1979.
13. New York Times, April 26, 1979.
14. New York Times, May 13, 1979.
15. Ibid.
16. Gaskin, Vol. I, Sunday Morning Services on the Farm, op. cit. supra., p. 8.
17. Hess. Letter to Martin Shepard (undated).
18. New York Times, May 3, 1979 L.I.
19. New York Times, May 6, 1979.
20. Suffolk Life, May 16, 1979.
21. 200 YEARS, Copyright 1973, U.S. News and World Report, Inc., Washington, D.C. 20037.
22. Ibid.
23. In a *special report* in *The New York Times* (December 1, 1979), Stephen Weisman reported that, according to Government estimates, it takes Americans 913 million hours to fill out 4,900 types of Federal reporting forms. This does not include state, city, county, township or village forms. The *report* further states that "President Carter, concerned that new environmental and energy laws might impose new reporting burdens on the public, signed an executive order to cut paperwork." Ironically, he continues, "Federal officials conceded that all this would actually increase Federal paperwork." According to Wayne G. Granquist, associate director of management and budget, "Whenever you try to put management controls on the Federal juggernaut, you wind up with some paper."
24. Reprinted from *Grit* (April 1, 1979, p. 4) with the permission of Grit Publishing Company, Williamsport, Pa. 17701.
25. New York Times, May 10, 1979.
26. Letter to Martin Shepard, undated.
27. See New York Times, May 3, 1979.

PROPOSITION 14

WHEREAS the various communities of The United States of America have been obliged to surrender their ability to live and to function freely, and

WHEREAS the individuals who live in these communities have been denied a meaningful say in the affairs of their common society, and

WHEREAS the two-party system, the electoral process, and the entire present system of governance have ceased to be either effective or responsive, and

WHEREAS the spirit of liberty still lives in the People, despite their victimization by those who manipulate government for personal power and gain, and

WHEREAS the Government has grown to such vast proportions that no one, however excellent and informed, can control or direct it,

THEREFORE, these communities according to the will of the individuals who constitute them, hereby reassert their autonomy:

To be free from the abuses of ever-increasing "government" in the form of usurpation of said communities' rightful function;

To end taxation beyond reasonable tolerance, and expenditure beyond any control;

To end the imposition of any form of harmful technology without due regard to the consequences.

These communities hereby declare themselves to be self-governing by direct democracy, which is the only system to further mankind and to preserve the world.